NEEDS, URGES, AND FEELINGS IN EARLY CHILDHOOD:

Helping Young Children Grow

NEEDS, URGES, AND FEELINGS IN EARLY CHILDHOOD:

Helping Young Children Grow

ERNA FURMAN

INTERNATIONAL UNIVERSITIES PRESS, INC.

Madison   Connecticut

Needs, Urges, and Feelings in Early Childhood: Helping Young Children Grow (ISBN 0-8236-8160-2)

The Library of Congress has catalogued the hardcover edition of this book as follows:

Library of Congress Cataloging in Publication Data

Furman, Erna.
    Helping young children grow.

    Bibliography: p.
    Includes index.
    1. Child development.   I. Title.
HQ767.9.F87   1987   649'.1   87-3196
ISBN 0-8236-2322-X

Manufactured in the United States of America

Contents

Preface

This paperback edition of *Helping Young Children Grow* (E. Furman, 1987a) differs from the earlier hardback in two respects: (1) It is divided into three volumes, representing Parts I, II, and III in the original, and titled accordingly *Relationships in Early Childhood* (E. Furman, 1998a), *Self-Control and Mastery in Early Childhood* (E. Furman, 1998b), and *Needs, Urges, and Feelings in Early Childhood*. The aim is to allow the reader to begin by focusing on the area of his or her special interest. (2) The references and related reading sections are updated.

    The Teacher's Guide to Helping Young Children Grow (E. Furman, 1987b), the companion book to the original edition, remains available as an important aid to those who are interested in using any or all volumes of *Helping Young Children Grow* as a textbook in teaching a child development–parenting course. This is the purpose for which the book was initially designed, and it has been used successfully with groups as diverse as high school, college, and medical students; educators and mental health professionals at all levels; parents of all ages; and, not least, teachers learning to teach such a course.

    The Teacher's Guide also describes how *Helping Young Children Grow* developed as a project of the Cleveland Center for Research in Child Development, the work of the research group, and the source and use of the data, that is, the scientific basis of the book. Beginning in 1974, the research group consisted of Elizabeth Daunton, Eleanor Fiedler, Robert A. Furman, M.D., Joan Rich, Ph.D., Arthur L. Rosenbaum, M.D., and myself. I am most appreciative of and thankful for the contributions of my colleagues. My gratitude extends also to Penny Friedman and Theodore B. Wiehe, Jr., the first teachers trained to teach this child development course. Their experiences and those of their students helped shape the final format and content of the book.

January 1998   Erna Furman

Introduction: How We Learn About Child Development

We learn most things either by taking in previously unknown facts or by marshaling what we already know within ourselves and thinking it through in such a way as to reach a new level of understanding. With both methods, the relationship with the teacher and his or her influence as a model play an important role. With the first way of learning, the teacher presents new facts; with the second way, he or she assists us in developing our own thinking—the Socratic method. In dialogues, Socrates' pupils struggled to formulate their ideas and he, as teacher, questioned their evidence, reasoning, and conclusions to help them note their mistakes and refine their understanding. The special enjoyment and sense of inner conviction we derive from this form of learning has not been lost through the millenia. Most of us can recall some experience with it and know how good it feels. One high school senior, participating in one of our child development courses, put it this way: "What I learned today was especially meaningful because I knew it for the first time, and yet it had been with me all along and been part of my daily experience without me realizing it."

In practice we usually combine both methods of learning. However well we utilize, and are helped to utilize, the knowledge that already lies within us, we still need to add new facts from without. However eager we are to take in new facts, to make them truly our own, we still need to fit them in with what we already know, so that new and old knowledge become a coherent whole and can serve us as a base for further

1

understanding and mastery. With some subjects, such as reading, history, and mathematics, we primarily tend to acquire new facts because, at least initially, we know little or nothing about them. Even in these fields, however, effective learning increasingly depends on our ability to use and develop what we know, to integrate new facts into our existing inner framework, and to build on it. Other subjects, and child development is among them, can never be learned simply by taking in new facts. One reason for this is that we are not novices. All of us have, through our own experiences, accumulated a body of knowledge in this field. Another reason is that this subject calls not only upon our intellect, but also involves our feelings, attitudes, and values. These have, in individual ways, molded our intellectual perception and understanding of child development in the past, and they continue to exercise a special influence on any additional learning we undertake.

In learning about child development, therefore, it is very necessary to draw on our available knowledge and to use it to develop and formulate our own better understanding. It is just as necessary to add new facts in a manner and at a pace which allow us to integrate them effectively.

This is not always easy. Insofar as the new facts are in accord with what we already think, feel, and know, we assimilate them readily. They are not totally foreign and may merely extend or deepen our prior knowledge. But when the new facts run counter to our own ideas, when they seem quite strange, and may even be felt as a threat, we cannot fit them into our own framework. How do our minds cope with this hurdle?

One way is to bury, or set aside, in ourselves all that we know, feel, and think, and to take in eagerly all the new knowledge that is available. We pile the newly presented facts on top of our previous experience without making the necessary inner confrontations and connections. But the new knowledge never truly becomes a part of ourselves. It remains isolated in our minds, fails to advance our real understanding, and cannot be applied to solving problems. We tend to forget it after a while, or set it aside as useless, and we look for a "newer," different body of knowledge, or we make do without. Gradually the old buried experience resurfaces and takes over the void. Most of us can recall taking a class in which we crammed in long lectures and whole bookfuls of new facts, but since we could never integrate them into our own life experience, we can now recover only meaningless relics or muddled dicta. Such has been the fate of many an erudite course or book on child development.

Another way is to reject the new, uncongenial facts outright in favor of our own knowledge. Freud said that education, government, and psychoanalysis—and we may add child development—comprise the most difficult professions because so many people consider themselves experts on the basis of their limited personal experience. All of us have indeed been educated and governed, and have experienced inner stress and turmoil. Most of us have also educated others, governed their lives to some extent, and helped them with their troubles, as parents, relatives, baby-sitters, friends, or even in one or another professional capacity. Regardless of whether we fared well or poorly, these experiences have been such an intimate part of our lives for as long as we can remember that we are apt to view them as a qualifying certificate. Sometimes we even believe that people are naturally endowed with expertise in these fields. Many a young mother and father have been too ashamed to admit their panicky helplessness in figuring out what their baby was crying for, or how to comfort him, because they thought that all other parents knew naturally the right thing to do. After all, "anybody knows what to do with a little kid," and therefore does not need to consider unsettling new knowledge. When we face newly presented facts about child development in this frame of mind, we can only reject them.

Is it possible to overcome these tendencies in ourselves and to make learning about child development more productive? There is a way, but it is hard, its pace is slow, and its extent depends on the individual makeup of the learner's personality. It consists of using the Socratic method of thinking through and formulating what we know within ourselves, and then adding new facts selectively, at times when we have pinpointed gaps in our knowledge and seek more information. As we contrast old and new facts and ideas, we may decide to revise some old knowledge, or we may find some of the new ideas unacceptable but can at least consider them thoughtfully. An active learning process gets under way. With the help of the newly marshaled and more clearly understood old knowledge we sample and test the new knowledge. Some of it is gradually and effectively linked and interwoven with what we already know, some is set aside, perhaps to remain unacceptable, perhaps to be mastered and integrated later. Sometimes this process of learning proceeds so smoothly and quietly that we hardly know we are learning at all. ("Why, I knew this all along.") Sometimes it leads to joyful moments of insight: "Ah, of course, so that's what it is!" And at other times it frustrates and angers us as we grapple with an unfamiliar idea, doubting or attacking it. The process does not end when the lesson ends, or even when the course ends. We keep mulling things over and reexamining them in the light of later experiences. The idea has become our own thing.

We have found this way of learning child development to be the most successful, although it is time consuming, arduous for both student and teacher, and not without some limitations. Several of us at the Cleveland Center for Research in Child Development have used this method since the early fifties with hundreds of professionals in the fields of health and education as well as with parents. Since 1976 it has been used with many more hundreds of senior high school students. However, all this work of teaching and learning, first without and later with the help of this book and its companion volumes (E. Furman, 1998a, 1998b), has involved personal contact between teachers and students, has utilized lively discussions between them, and has been facilitated by their close working relationship, as described in the *Teacher's Guide* (E. Furman, 1987b).

Can a writer and reader work together in a similar fashion? I trust we can. This volume tries to approximate the same way of teaching, to reach out to you, the interested reader, and to engage your active participation. Your task is not an easy one. It is indeed much more difficult than that of the learner in the classroom. How you go about it and to what extent you use the material is up to you. My good wishes accompany you in your endeavor, and I offer a few suggestions: Before you begin to read a chapter, take time to think about the topic yourself. What do you think and feel about it? Can you relate your ideas to specific situations you have observed or experienced? Do these situations confirm your opinions or are they at odds with them in some instances? What might be the reasons? Perhaps you can figure them out and resolve any discrepancies to your own satisfaction. Perhaps you have even increased your understanding and, like one of my past students, can say, "When you are first asked to figure out your own answers you sort of feel you can't do that and you don't know what to think or say. But once you give it a go, it's really so easy and it all comes so naturally, like finding the pieces of a puzzle and suddenly it all fits. It's fun." Perhaps your puzzle pieces did not fit together and you are left annoyed, with bits and pieces of ideas that don't match. In either case, your efforts will pay off. They may help you to consider and evaluate the written text. Maybe its thoughts and examples will fit in with what you know, maybe they will look at the topic from a different angle, maybe they will seem strange and offer no solutions. Before you decide to accept or reject them, test them out. Observe closely children you know in your work or home, and children you don't know but encounter by chance in the street, supermarket, bus, at the movies, wherever. See whether your observations shed more light on the topic. If you feel sufficiently comfortable with some of the approaches described in the book, try them out and see how they work. You may not feel happy with your effort or with the results, but you will at least gain more food for thought.

When you have worked through a topic, ask yourself what you remember of it, how it related to your experiences with children, what seemed important to you, and what else you would like to know about it.

Regardless of whether you could use all, some, or none of what the book offered, your own mental work will have helped you to see the issues more clearly, to marshal your own thinking and experience, and to pinpoint areas of uncertainty. Perhaps the discussion of the next or later topics will prove helpful, when themes reappear in new contexts or when new ideas illuminate previously presented ones. Your own thinking, like the chapters, weaves to and fro and makes connections. Although the various aspects of child development are arranged in a sequence which facilitates learning, do not hesitate to skip around, to read later chapters, or parts of chapters, first. You may, in this way, want to link an earlier topic with a later one, or you may just be interested in another aspect. In class discussions topics are often interwoven and aspects are taken up "out of order," in keeping with the students' observations, questions, and thoughts. It is your book; use it in the way which you feel best suits your interests. And don't forget that there are two more volumes—*Relationships in Early Childhood* (E. Furman, 1998a) and *Self-Control and Mastery in Early Childhood* (E. Furman, 1998b). Both may help you to tie up loose ends, to get a feel for personality growth as a coherent whole.

Obviously, these books are not intended to impose on you or to convince you. They are neither a big meal you should swallow whole, nor authoritarian dicta you should bow to and believe. Understanding how children develop and mature is a lifelong quest to get to know and appreciate our fellow humans and a part of ourselves. Let us proceed with respect and good will.

1

How the Child Channels Life's Energies Into Well-being, Enjoyment of Activities, and Emotional Growth

In *Relationships in Early Childhood* (E. Furman, 1998a) we talked about the personal ties which are so crucial to the child's survival and growth and about the ways in which the parents and other caring adults facilitate the unfolding of the child's personality and help him to cope with the world. In *Self-Control and Mastery in Early Childhood* (E. Furman, 1998b) we focused on when and how a child gets to be master of himself, developing and using his personality tools to cope with daily tasks, and acquiring the kind of self-esteem and conscience that enable him to do so in a self-disciplined and satisfying manner. We will discuss here the inner forces that give us "go," impel us to want and do things, and to search out ways of getting them. People use different terms for the momentum of life but we all recognize that, like all other living beings, we are endowed with energy that radiates from within us, fuels our strivings for preserving life, and gives impetus to the building and maintaining of our personalities. This energy manifests itself in needs and urges which we seek to relieve and gratify, and in feelings which are associated with them. Needs, urges, and feelings are always closely connected but they do not remain the same throughout life. At different developmental levels they vary considerably in nature and intensity, and the growing child experiences and deals with them in different ways. Before we look at each more closely, let us clarify for ourselves what we mean by "needs, urges, and feelings," how they work together, and what part they play in the child's development.

7

WHAT ARE NEEDS, URGES, AND FEELINGS?

Our basic *needs* are bodily. They arise from hunger, thirst, elimination, fatigue, and pain. As the baby grows, other needs emerge as well, such as the need for activity, the need for protection and safety, the need for a loving, caring adult, and for companionship. Needs do not change; they are always with us and always have to be met. However, their intensity varies (for example, children are more hungry during spurts of bodily growth and/or when they are very active) and we also learn to satisfy them in ways that are acceptable in our community (for example, we learn to eat certain foods, use certain table manners, limit ourselves to eating at mealtimes).

The energies that manifest themselves as *urges* differ from needs in that they change in the course of development, can be transformed, diverted to serve different ends, and gratified in a variety of ways. We experience urges in their basic forms but can also be helped to put their energy to use in many activities in our daily lives. The energy of urges is so versatile that I find it helpful to think of it as though it were a river. Its source is in ever-gushing springs and all along its course it provides for our use and enjoyment. We swim, boat, and fish in it, we draw its water to drink and grow food, we use it to ship our goods. But its flow also carries potential danger—flooding and drowning. Yet by channeling the river's waters, by damming and piping them, we can tame their forces, widen and enhance their usefulness, transform them into electricity, and make them into a vital asset to many communities. In a similar way, our urges are neither good nor bad. They are there and it all depends on how we use them. Urges (also called drives, impulses, or instincts) may be viewed as twofold (A. Freud, 1949b):

1. The pleasure seeking urges are perceived in different bodily parts and we experience them as excitement or sexuality. The mouth, the anus and buttocks, the skin, the genitals are the main focus of these urges at different developmental stages. In time, the pleasure seeking urges are also channeled and invested in interests and activities that are no longer connected with specific body parts. The pleasure we derive from sports, playing, working, hobbies, and learning is still

full of zest and fun, but it is less intense and immediate than the bodily excitement. On the other hand, it lasts longer and enriches the whole personality. For example, young children's excitement in looking at each other's bodies and their curiosity about sexual functions later motivates them to learn about other things and to enjoy finding out how they work and why.

2. The aggressive urges, in their most primitive form, aim to destroy. In the earliest phases of the child's development they manifest themselves in screaming, biting, and in physically hurting people and things. Very soon, however, they also come to play a helpful and important part in furthering the child's zest for life. When we do not get what we want we feel angry and summon our aggressive energy to clear the obstacles that stand in our way. When something or someone threatens our personal safety and well-being we get angry and use our aggressive energy to defend ourselves. In these ways aggressive energy serves us to fulfill our needs and to gratify the pleasures we seek. As the child matures, aggressive urges are modified so that they can serve without causing actual harm; for example, angry words of protest take the place of hurting actions.

Almost from the start, however, aggressive urges are also transformed into activity and channeled into pursuits that retain the original impulse "to do" without the destructive goal. The same energy that fueled the angry screaming of the baby and the provocative kicking of the toddler later contributes to the older child's ability to work with a hammer, to excel in sports. It may ultimately even help him to become a skilled surgeon. Mental activities also require much of that determined activity, in learning and in working. Our language reminds us of this with phrases like "tackling a task," "grappling with a problem." And in elementary school, children are graded in "word attack," a part of learning to spell. In the form of activities and pursuits, aggressive urges contribute a great deal to personality growth and adaptation.

Feelings alert us to our needs and urges and let us know whether and how they are satisfied. Our memory of pleasurable and unpleasurable feelings leads us to want to repeat, change, or avoid the experiences that gave rise to them. The baby's feelings are very intense and very simple. Through them he perceives comfort and discomfort, pleasure and pain. By the end of the first year of life, and increasingly during the preschool years, the child acquires a wider range of feelings and they become more subtle and finely differentiated in tone—love, hate, sadness, happiness, envy, helplessness, anger, fear, jealousy, loneliness, delight, disappointment enjoyment, fondness, shame, embarrassment, pity, guilt, and many more. The child also develops a greater capacity for recognizing them, tolerating them, expressing them in word and thought instead of action, and using them to understand himself and others. In this way feelings are essential to helping us know what goes on within ourselves and what to do about it. At the same time, they enable us to feel with others, to recognize true friend and foe, to know when to trust and when to beware.

HOW NEEDS, URGES, AND FEELINGS
WORK TOGETHER

A healthy baby is born with the need of hunger. He feels discomfort when he is hungry, makes sucking and searching movements with his mouth, and readily "learns" how to draw food from a nipple. When the uncomfortable feeling gives way to a comfortable one, his hunger is stilled and he stops drinking. Nature reinforces such an important need as hunger by giving it a companion. During the first year of life a large share of the pleasure seeking urge is located in the lips and mouth, so that all the mouth activities are experienced as stimulating and exciting, provide intense pleasure, and are eagerly sought out. Touching with the mouth, sucking and drinking satisfy hunger as well as these early pleasure seeking urges. As the baby remembers the good feelings they generate, he builds the idea that eating is fun. This helps him to want to eat again and again.

Within a few months, when the teeth begin to grow and prepare the infant for chewing food, the aggressive urges too join in this new mouth activity. Chewing and biting on hard objects relieves teething discomfort, is soon used in eating solid foods, and helps the baby to enjoy new foods and new ways of eating. This blend of hunger, pleasurable excitement, and aggressive activity serves the baby's self-preservation. To an extent, it remains with us all through life, even when the mouth is no longer the main site of pleasure and aggression, when other parts of the body have become more exciting and gratifying, and when aggression and activity are expressed in new ways. As adults we still enjoy eating and chewing, but at times when we are temporarily deprived of these satisfactions we really appreciate just how much they mean to us; for example, a liquid diet or intravenous feeding may provide us with all the necessary nutrients but none of the fun. We get to feeling low and irritable and long for real mouthfuls of crunchy food, "something to sink your teeth into." When babies cannot derive sufficient pleasurable excitement from eating (perhaps due to illness or inadequate handling of their feeding by the mother) and/or when they cannot use biting and chewing in eating (perhaps because they are fed soft babyfoods instead of food to hold and chew on their own), their appetite is diminished. They become poor eaters and may not thrive well. Their early lack of zest in eating may also affect later developments which, as we shall see, are connected with the use of the mouth.

The baby's mouth pleasure exists also separately from eating. Babies suck their tongues, thumbs, fingers, or other objects even when they are not hungry, just for the fun of it, and they also use this kind of sucking to comfort themselves, to counteract and alleviate stress and pain. Some of this use of the mouth continues later on. It becomes a part of adult sexuality in the form of kissing, for example, and may be used for comfort even by grown-ups, such as when drinking and eating without hunger or smoking. Similarly, aggressive mouth urges surface independently of hunger. Babies scream and bite in anger. In later life too, chewing can serve to discharge aggression or irritability; for example, some of us use food or gum "to chew our little troubles away."

Soon, however, the urges already invested in the mouth in connection with eating come to play a part in a newly developing mouth activity—talking. Babbling and forming words is, in part, motivated by the sheer fun of using the mouth. Infants who have not experienced enough urge satisfaction in feeding are slower to vocalize and may never get to enjoy speech, but those who have relished their eating readily transfer the mouth pleasure they have felt to the new mouth activity. Making sounds, ever new and different sounds, is very exciting for the baby and toddler. As adults we still like to talk and sorely miss it when we don't get enough chance to talk, but our feelings about talking are more subtle. Some of us can come close to empathizing with the very young child's thrill when we can at least recall what fun it was in later childhood to pronounce new big words, to roll off the likes of "antidisestablishmentarianism," or to savor as catchy a mouthful as "supercalifragilisticexpialidocious" from the famous Mary Poppins' song. Anger too takes its place in speech. It may take the form of very sophisticated and contained verbal expression of annoyance or anger, but may also show in yelling, in "chewing someone out," or in "biting sarcasm."

Quite early on the bodily taking in of food is also channeled into mental taking in, a less direct satisfaction. When babies' needs and urges are satiated, their energy becomes more and more available for interest in their environment. Babies "hunger" for stimuli after the first few weeks and "greedily take in" or even "devour" people and things with their eyes, ears, and other senses. Whatever they can reach and grab, they bring into their mouths to explore, taste, learn about. In time, the basic bodily excitement and aggression in taking in become a more refined mental pleasure and activity. In this channeled form, taking in is an important part of all learning. It fuels it with motivation, pleasure, and persistence and gives rise to many subtle associated feelings. In psychoanalytic treatment, many children's learning difficulties can be traced to early problems with taking in by mouth or to obstacles in channeling the bodily mouth excitement and aggression into the mental pleasure and activity of learning.

Even the child's wish and ability to "take in," to "incorporate," traits and values from the loved caring adults are, in part, based on the early bodily urges connected with eating. As the growing child's primitive taking-in urges are newly channeled, they motivate the mental taking in of parental attributes and help build the child's personality. Yes, a good feed does a lot more for a baby than keeping him alive.

HOW THE ENVIRONMENT AFFECTS OUR NEEDS, URGES, AND FEELINGS AND HELPS US TO SATISFY AND CHANNEL THEM

Children are born with their rich heritage of life's energies but they have only a very limited ability to know them, to satisfy them on their own, and to regulate and channel them to best advantage for their well-being and personality growth.

At first the parents recognize and meet the child's needs and help him satisfy his urges. However, from the start, they also assist the child to become aware of them himself, to communicate and cope with them. They go about this task in many ways.

The most basic and important way is being in tune with the child. The mothering person, and later both parents, sense what their youngster feels, needs, and wants. When they are with him most of the time, when they are emotionally close to him, and when they are in good touch with their own feelings, they are able to empathize (that is, sense correctly the child's feelings and feel with him). The parent's knowing not only helps him or her to do right by the child, it also paves the way for the child getting to know what goes on inside himself. Babies but a few months old at once look at the mother when they experience a strong feeling, pleasant or unpleasant. Her facial expression, body posture, and perhaps contact with the infant's body helps them to feel that she understands them, that she can tolerate and contain whatever it is they feel, that it is okay and will somehow work out. If mother is distraught or unresponsive, the baby does not feel understood, becomes bewildered, distressed, or panicky.

Most mothers talk with their babies. They put their understanding of the infant into words, "Oh boy, are you hungry?"; "My, you're real angry, aren't you?"; "You are so sleepy."; "Oh, that thumb tastes good."; "You're getting all excited in the water; it's fun." The infants, in turn, understand mothers' words long before they can talk. As we already know, when children get to know the word, the *name* for what they are experiencing, they can take a big step toward tolerating the inner sensations. When children don't know what they feel and can't think about it in words, their feelings can't serve them well. To children they seem like an inside turmoil that may grow so big and intense that it overwhelms them (as in a temper tantrum); or that may propel them blindly to do things that bring them more trouble than satisfaction (as in grabbing things that could hurt); or that get them into the wrong situation altogether (as when they don't recognize that they are ill and get irritable and mean to others instead of asking them for help and comfort). As children begin to use words, they can also communicate their needs, wants, and feelings to mother and others, which is a further big step toward taking care of themselves (Katan, 1961; Hall, 1982b; E. Furman, 1992, 1993).

Just as it helps the child when the parents know what he feels and when they name it correctly for him, so it also helps when they do for it whatever may be appropriate. Their ministrations, their ways of providing pleasure or comfort and relief, let the child know what he can do for himself; the toddler already knows to get the cookie tin when he is hungry, or to hug his teddy when he is lonely.

The parents also help by allowing the child to gain pleasure and comfort in ways that are age appropriate and natural for him, that he need not learn from them; for example, they let him suck his thumb or fingers, and they take care that his "blankie" does not get washed lest it lose its precious smell.

Gradually, they add to their handling new ways of coping which involve control and mastery. They begin to expect that their child delay satisfactions and accept partial or substitute gratifications. We discussed elsewhere (E. Furman, 1998b) how parents assist their child in developing and enjoying some of his own inner means of control and mastery: Speech and thinking help him to know what he feels, to express it in words for partial relief, to plan and choose what he will do, and to postpone real action; motility enables him to do, and frustration tolerance helps him not to do. Usually parents also wait until the child can enjoy new pleasures before they ask him to give up old ones; for example, the fun of feeding himself can take the place of nursing from breast or bottle, and parents expect the young child not to hit and kick when he begins to talk and can *say* that he is angry.

From early on too, parents help the child to channel his urges, to divert them from bodily to nonbodily or neutral activities and satisfactions; for example, they don't let the toddler play with his urine and bowel movements but join his fun in water play at the sink and in the tub with toys, or they help him dig in the sandbox. Much of that play is "messing" too, but it is a step away from the body and a step toward such creative activities as modeling with clay and painting pictures.

All these are difficult and slow developmental steps and the child's success or failure depends a lot on the way the parents go about helping him—their timing, their preparation of the child for new expectations and new opportunities for expression, their pleasure in his tiniest accomplishment, their patience with his slowness and inevitable setbacks. Much of the time, parent and child work together toward the same goals; for example, a child who has really enjoyed his nursing months is eager to reach for the new pleasure of self-feeding and joining the family meal. Similarly, most toddlers don't mind much, and gladly help, when mother quickly removes their dirty diapers and they enjoy, almost as much, splashing around with their toys in the bath by way of getting clean. But there are always times when parents and child want very different things, such as when the child wants to pull the cat's tail and the parents stop him and expect him to be "nice to the poor kitty," or when junior wants to sleep with Mom and Dad and they insist that he stay in his own bed. How these conflicts are resolved, what disciplinary measures the parents use, and how the child is helped gradually to take into himself the parents' attitudes has a lot to do with their relationship and with the building of mental self-esteem and conscience (E. Furman, 1998a, 1998b). Much of the important foundation for coping with needs, urges, and feelings is laid at home, in the preschool years. During this period the parents' handling helps the child's personality to allow proper room and scope for his inner energies so that they can serve him well (E. Furman, 1992, 1993).

WHEN DO NEEDS, URGES, AND FEELINGS HELP AND WHEN DO THEY HINDER?

Some parents feel at odds with the child's needs, urges, and feelings. They do not trust that they can help the child to live with them and make every effort to control, oppose, or banish them as though they were enemies or competitors for the child's allegiance. They may think that children would never want to sleep or sleep enough unless made to, or that they would always stay in bed too late and get lazy unless they interfere; they control the meals as though children would never eat unless they had to, or would only eat the wrong foods, or would eat too much. Likewise they assume that children will indulge their bodily pleasures unless altogether forbidden to do so (for example, that they will always suck their thumbs if permitted to do so in infancy), and that the children's anger at the parents will destroy their loving feelings if they are ever allowed to express anger.

Their children may ultimately conform, may take over the parental attitudes, but at a cost. They may feel at odds with themselves, may need to restrict their zest in living, their ability to satisfy and enjoy themselves, and to pursue a variety of interests and activities. They may feel burdened with guilt and shame over the slightest indulgence or develop neurotic symptoms, the overt signs of inner conflict. However, there are many other possible outcomes; for example, the parents' prophecy may become self-fulfilling and the children may, secretly or in open rebellion, resist the excessive parental restrictions and follow the dictates of their feelings, needs, and urges. That does not necessarily spare them conflict and misgiving, nor does it enable them to put their endowment to their own best use.

By contrast, other parents feel that the child's feelings, needs, and urges should be given free reign and expression. They permit, even encourage, the child to follow his inclination of the moment wherever and whenever, sometimes in the hope that sufficient discharge will enable the child to "get it out of his system." This too does not lead to happiness. The children may come to feel unprotected and overwhelmed, at the mercy of their impulses, without means of mastery. They may fail to learn to consider their safety, to channel their drives into rewarding activities, or to fit them in with the standards of their community. This may create inner dread and outer conflict instead of satisfaction.

For better or worse, it is not possible to get rid of needs, urges, and feelings. We can neither push them under and deny them all gratification, nor can we expect them to redirect or exhaust themselves by allowing them unlimited gratification, nor can we really enjoy them if we do. It is only when we learn to use them wisely that we have a chance to use them well, so that they can help preserve and enrich our lives. Individuals and societies vary greatly in the kind of satisfactions they endorse, and when, where, and in what form they allow them to take place. However, there is no individual and no society, primitive or advanced, that can live and thrive without permitting some gratifications and without imposing some restrictions. It is the balance between them that counts, and it is their infinitely varied combination which is largely responsible for the many differences between individuals and between societal customs and mores. In each case it is initially the parents who influence the outcome.

ARE THE AGGRESSIVE URGES REALLY INNATE OR ARE THEY A RESPONSE TO FRUSTRATIONS?

Anger is indeed observed most frequently and clearly as a response to frustration. This may lead us to assume that anger arises *only* in connection with frustration. Whether or not this is really so is one part of the question; the other part deals with whether it is innate. Let us look at this latter part first.

When we say that a child "responds" with anger, we may mean one of two things: either that we are made in such a way that we get angry when frustrated (in which case our anger is part of our makeup, that is, innate) or that we learn to be angry when frustrated (in which case we mean not only that we would not get angry if we were never frustrated, but also that we would not get angry unless we were taught this kind of response to frustration). Unfortunately, no life can proceed without any frustration. From early on, everyone is faced with at least some frustrations, like not being able to stick our fingers into electric outlets. This makes it impossible to test how a total lack of frustration would affect our feelings. Given the fact, then, that there are always some frustrations we have much opportunity to observe that children do not have to be taught to respond to them with anger. Even during their first year, babies scream and bite angrily, and parents of toddlers are never in doubt that their youngsters know how to be angry even when they have not experienced the example of their parents' anger at them. There are few, if any, people who believe that anger is an acquired response, taught like table manners or like a conditioned reflex, by association through repeated experience.

Let us now turn to the other part of the question, whether anger is felt only in frustrating situations. Some years ago, when it became known that excessive frustrations make young children very angry, many educators hoped that we could greatly reduce children's anger if we kept their frustrations to a minimum. They gratified children's wishes as much as possible, made few demands on them, and adapted the environment to their needs. The children they thus raised became not less, but more angry. The least little frustration infuriated them. Obviously, relative lack of frustrations had not diminished their anger. It had merely diminished their chances of learning how to cope with difficult situations. They were as helplessly angry at small frustrations as the excessively frustrated children had been helplessly angry at big ones. Both were unable to use their anger as an impetus to purposeful activity because for each, though for different reasons, the frustrating situations were beyond their means of mastery.

A number of other experiences favor a view of aggression as an urge rather than as a mere reaction to frustration. Among these are many observations of young children's spontaneous unprovoked manifestations of anger, such as maltreatment of pets and other animals who had neither harmed nor threatened them. Also, we have learned from the psychoanalytic treatment of inactive children that their difficulties resulted from aggression not being channeled into appropriate personality functions; for example, some children could not chew food, could not be bodily active in sports, could not defend themselves and their belongings, could not learn with zest and "tackle" problems until therapy helped them to reach their early suppressed aggression and to tap its energy for use (see also chapter 4).

We need to keep in mind, however, that the concept of aggression as an urge is not a religious dogma, to be believed unquestioningly. Like any other scientific formulation, it is merely a convenient framework for relating and understanding the available data in a comprehensive, logical manner. When new observations defy explanation within a given theoretical framework, it is time to change it. This may, some day, happen to the concept of aggression as an urge.

DO KIDS HAVE THE SAME FEELINGS AS GROWN-UPS?

As we have mentioned, during the first few months of life, babies' feelings are more on the lines of "good" and "bad," but after that they become more varied and are indeed like those of the adult. There are some differences: One is the young child's very limited means of tolerating and mastering feelings, so that he always experiences them as very intense, even overwhelming; the other is that every person feels most strongly about the things that matter most to him or her individually. The things that matter most to a child depend on his level of development and on his personal experiences. These are not necessarily the same as those of a grown-up; for example, not being with his mother and feeling that she is irretrievably gone arouses very strong feelings in a young child but may not be of much concern to the adult, who would feel a comparable feeling if he were to lose his job, spouse, and children. Of course adults too differ in the kinds of things they feel strongly about and in their ability to cope with feelings.

2
Needs

Many people assume that our basic needs (hunger and thirst, sleep, elimination) are so crucial to survival that they must assert themselves spontaneously and that we must be equipped with ways of meeting them. Surely babies know how to sleep when they are tired, how to eat and drink when they are hungry and thirsty (well, at least drink), and how to urinate and pass bowel movements. And, if it is true that pleasure-seeking and aggressive urges support these needs and participate in their satisfactions, then there is even more reason to think that needs present no problem for the child or adult.

Yet, when we take a closer look at the way things work out in life, we begin to doubt such an opinion: Babies know how to eat but not how to get food; toddlers eat stones and paint and even bowel movements but often refuse good foods, like stew and vegetables; older children sometimes eat much more than their bodies need so that they become obese, or they starve themselves, even to death (as happens in anorexia nervosa). Most parents complain, at one time or another, that their children eat too much, too little, the "wrong" foods, at the wrong time. They may also complain that their children do not learn to satisfy their hunger independently, that they want to be spoon-fed, that they don't want to fix their school lunch to take along, or help with preparing meals at home.

The need for sleep does not fare much better. Some children won't go to bed, or can't fall asleep, or won't sleep in their own beds. Many parents complain that their preschoolers wake up too early, that their teenagers sleep in too late, or that their children at any age "never get enough sleep." Many adults too are beset by sleep problems of one kind or another. Elimination is, likewise, a frequent source of difficulties. Some children soil their pants or wet their beds until they are quite old, others hold back bowel movements for days or wriggle and squirm instead of urinating.

In fact, children and even grown-ups manifest such frequency and variety of interferences in being able to recognize and meet their needs that many people go to the opposite extreme. They feel that there is nothing innate that prompts us to sense what is good for us or how to satisfy it. Acting on this assumption, parents then hold themselves responsible for prescribing what their children need and enforcing that they do as they are told: what and how much to eat, when to sleep and for how long, when to use the toilet and how much to produce.

In this area of child development, as in most, it is unrealistic and unhelpful to think in terms of extremes. So where is the true middle line? We have actually looked at it a bit already in connection with one need, the need for bodily safety (E. Furman, 1998b). There we saw that children are normally endowed with a physiological pain barrier. When a newborn or very young baby is subjected to discomforts that exceed the limit set by the pain barrier, he experiences uncomfortable feelings and responds with discharges which serve as protest and SOS signals—crying, screaming, squirming, kicking, and hand waving. But we have also seen that this innate "security system" does not protect the infant adequately and does not automatically develop into a serviceable means of meeting his need for safety. Initially a mothering person has to be available who responds to her baby's signals, gauges what is wrong, and knows how to put it right. If she fulfills this task consistently and lovingly she enables her infant to feel good often, to get to know and like his body, to seek out states of pleasurable, safe well-being, and to avoid and protest pain. In other words, the mother's protective activity helps to link the innate pain barrier with the pleasure-seeking urges and to channel the aggressive urges into the service of self-defense. In this way she facilitates the process by which need and urges form a stronger and more effective mental pain barrier than the physiological distress of need alone could provide.

Nor is this all the parent helps accomplish. Then come the long years during which the parental know-how of meeting the need for safety is gradually handed over to the growing child. A number of things can go wrong along the way. For example, the child's innate need for safety and properly developed wish to avoid discomfort may not suffice to protect him from dangers he cannot yet assess (like not knowing yet about hot stoves); or his innate need for safety may be interfered with and altogether "overruled" when he does not experience enough bodily pleasure (as may happen with neglected or abused children who cease to protest against pain and may even seek out hurts). The innate need for safety is there and it does assert itself from the start but, in the course of development, it has to be joined by other forces within the personality, and it has to be tended carefully from without; only then can it come to serve us well and only then can we learn to meet it adequately. The parents' role is crucial, but the mere fact that they and their relationship with the child have so much to do with the whole process can also make for difficulties (E. Furman, 1984b, 1992, 1993).

We can similarly follow the developmental paths of the other needs and the ways in which they may be facilitated or interfered with.

RESPECTING NEEDS

Perhaps the parents' most helpful attitude to their child's needs is respect: "My child's needs are a part of his precious life force. They are the essence of his being alive. They are truly his and it is our job to help him use them for himself to his best advantage." Of course, parents are not likely to spell this out for themselves in so many words, but many parents feel it and act on it. So, the first thing they do is to learn and understand the initially primitive ways in which their baby signals his needs and they create an environment in which he can attain satisfaction.

The mother, or primary caregiver, watches out for her baby's hunger signs, tries to gauge them from his behavior, from her knowledge of his feeding rhythm, and, if she breast-feeds her baby, from the fullness of her breasts, because her milk production is geared to the baby's hunger. When she gauges his signals accurately and offers him the appropriate food in a comfortable way, he will take it in. Mother will watch and get to know her baby's own ways of eating—slowly, fast, or intermittently with stops and starts. When he has had enough he will stop eating altogether and mother will find out how he acts when his hunger and thirst are satisfied—perhaps he goes to sleep, or stretches and yawns, or starts looking around, or wriggling around, or he may just like to lie relaxed. In the beginning she may misjudge his signals of hunger (perhaps change his diapers instead of offering him food) and she will learn from his responses whether she guessed right. She will also show her respect by recognizing that he is sometimes more and sometimes less hungry and allow his hunger to decide how much he needs to eat. Later, when she introduces additional foods, she will respect his taste and give him time to get used to new tastes. She will offer a little of just one new food and see how he likes it. If he doesn't, she may wait a few days and offer it again, or she may try another food, or she may change the taste of the first food by adding sugar or spice to make it more palatable. In short, her respect tells her that her baby's hunger "knows" when, what, and how much is good for him and will assert itself unless she violates it and interferes with it too much.

In the same way the mother learns her baby's signals for needing sleep, the ways in which he can best go to sleep and sleep well. For example, he may need quiet holding, or gentle rocking, or a crib or wall decoration to look at, he may need low lights or darkness, he may be bothered by the banging of doors or other noises. She watches for the times and places that help him sleep and tries to arrange her schedule accordingly; for example, if his crib and room are the best place, she plans her errands with him at "awake" periods. She also watches out for the ways in which he shows that his need for sleep has been satisfied—perhaps when he wakes up gurgling, playing with his hands, looking around. In this way she knows whether he is really slept out or had his sleep interrupted—perhaps by a commotion in the house, by being hungry, or having a tummy ache—in which case he will need to sleep again after the interference has been taken care of.

When it comes to elimination, the baby is usually able to complete the whole cycle on his own, from need signal to *relieving* himself, the word aptly describing both the expulsion of urine and feces and the good feeling of relief or satisfaction that follows it. The mother's help is needed only for cleaning up afterwards. But with this need too, she observes her infant's signals, how his face reddens as he squirms and twists, how he relaxes and smiles when he is done and ready to be cleaned. She gets to know his natural rhythm, whether he has several stools a day or one every other day, whether they tend to be looser or harder. She respects his ways, such as by not trying to feed him when he is busy straining for a bowel movement. And when, at a time of minor illness, upset, or change in diet, her child is made uncomfortable by constipation or diarrhea, mother tries to assist his body with gentle means and refrains from interfering and taking over; for example, she may offer him fruit juices to soften his stools or mashed banana to harden them, rather than introducing purgatives, suppositories, or enemas that produce uncomfortably intense feelings and deprive the child of his bodily mastery.

This may all sound as if it takes the patience of Job and every minute of the day, but most mothers do it as a matter of course. One reason is that they enjoy it, as they enjoy most things about their babies, another reason is that they know it pays off. A baby whose needs are not heeded becomes cranky and irritable and is much harder to take care of.

When the mother comes to know well her infant's need signals and can help him become satisfied, the baby soon learns which feelings go with different needs and with different satisfactions. Within a few weeks or months, for example, a baby's hunger cry becomes specific and easily differentiated from other need signals, and he usually calms down as soon as the appropriate need-satisfying procedures are under way, such as when mother shows him the bottle, or when she starts the going-to-sleep routine, or when she lays him down to change his diapers. Now *he* knows when he is hungry, or tired, or uncomfortably wet and dirty, and can let mother know. When this happens, mother and child have accomplished an important step in helping him to meet his own needs: His feelings of comfort and discomfort are no longer indiscriminate. He has begun to recognize his own needs, to know what it takes to satisfy them, and how it feels when they are satisfied. This will stand him in good stead as he grows older and becomes more independent. Even an adult's taking good care of his needs always involves respecting them, knowing what they are, what to do for them, doing all he can to satisfy them, and getting help if need be. The mother's respect and understanding of her child's needs becomes, in time, the child's and adult's own attitude to himself.

DOING FOR HIMSELF

As the mother lays the groundwork of respecting her child's needs, the next steps are also under way: helping the child to become more and more proficient at doing for himself and at asking for assistance with what he can't do for himself. From the very start, the mother usually allows her baby to be as active as possible in meeting his own needs and watches all along for signs that he is ready for new ways of participating and for taking over more of the "doing" that is involved in attaining satisfaction. For example, during the second half of the first year, many babies become restless at the breast, may grab hold more persistently of the bottle and spoon, try to put things in their mouths. Mother sees these and other little changes in behavior as signs that her infant wants to feed himself. So she allows him to begin to wean himself, offers him foods he can hold, suck, and chew on. Self-feeding has started. During the same period she may notice that her earlier rocking and holding no longer help her baby with falling asleep. In fact, it may make him a little "wound up." But he calms and closes his eyes when he lies on his own, sucking his fingers, and perhaps rubbing his ear or blanket. In short, he is ready to put himself to sleep and knows how to soothe himself with his own body and blanket or soft toy. So mother gradually phases out her part, substitutes a little kiss-and-pat good night routine, and lets him do the rest on his own.

Likewise, she will let him take part in the cleaning procedure. She lets him hold the sponge or washcloth and, as he begins to toddle, she may let him bring the clean diapers and open and shut the pail to soak the dirty ones. Many mothers allow their child to stand up when they clean and change them because they notice that the child dislikes lying passively on his back (R. A. Furman, 1991).

The mother also talks to her baby more now and gives him words for his needs: "You're sleepy. It's night-night time."; "Boy are you hungry! Dinner coming up!"; "That's a hard BM today. You are really working at it."; "Let's get off these diapers. You'll soon feel clean and comfy." In his second year, the toddler will begin to use some of these words himself, tell mother when he is hungry, and ask for cookies, juice, or whatever. How often mothers encourage a child: "I can't understand what you want when you scream and cry, tell me!"

Actually, children whose needs have been respected, who have enjoyed need satisfaction, and have been allowed to be active participants do not have to be made to want to do for themselves. They are very eager to take every possible new step toward independence and enjoy their accomplishments. And although mothers may miss their children's dependence, may miss being needed, they also appreciate the pleasures of their children's newly acquired know-how and enjoy it with them. The first steps may seem very small, but each is very important and leads to the next one, continuing throughout the growing years.

In learning to take care of his hunger, the child will go from self-feeding to helping himself to foods, to helping mother with shopping and cooking. Later he will also learn to anticipate getting hungry, will perhaps prepare his own luncheon sandwich and remember to take it along to school. And when he is close to being adult, he will buy his food and make sure he has sufficient supplies on hand. He will earn money and budget it to be able to buy his food. All along there will be times when he will have to enlist the help of others—with preparing and buying food, with money for food, with finding a job to earn money to buy food and, even when he is grown up, there may be times of illness or poverty when he will need to ask others for the kind of help he needed as a little child.

In taking care of his need for rest and sleep, the child will go from falling asleep with the help of his thumb or "blankie" to holding and playing with his teddy bear, to reading, or listening to the radio. He will learn to get ready for sleep on his own and will even tuck himself in. In time he will plan his daily activities so as to anticipate his need for sleep and allow enough time for it. Younger children often ask for help: "I'm tired."; "Mom, run my bath."; "Mom, come and kiss me good night." Older ones do not, unless they are ill or in unusual circumstances, such as when they can't use their usual room or bed.

And in taking care of his elimination, the child will progress from helping mother to clean him, to letting her know in words when he needs to be cleaned, to using the toilet on his own and cleaning himself. In time he will learn to plan for this need too, will go to the toilet before an outing or at recess between lessons, will find a bathroom before his need gets too urgent, and will fit it all smoothly into his daily routines and activities (E. Furman, 1992, 1993).

But is it all such easy going? Of course not. Mothers may not gauge the right times and ways for letting children do for themselves, and children contribute their share by either not wanting to take over their own care and demanding to be done for, or by wanting to be independent prematurely, insisting on doing things they can't yet do safely and well. Minor conflicts over dependence/independence arise often and can be resolved ("You can't serve the soup but you can serve the cookies."; "I won't undress you, but I'll be here and help with the hard T-shirt."; "Soon you'll know how to turn on the hot water on your own"). Major ongoing conflicts may interfere with the child's ability to take over need fulfillment. For example, many older children are not eager to do for themselves and do not enjoy it when they have to. This may happen when they were dissatisfied and felt deprived of mother's bodily care, or when their earlier attempts at independence were not appreciated. They then continue to demand care, resent self-care, and even neglect their needs or meet them inappropriately.

HELPING THE URGES TO PLAY THEIR PROPER PART IN NEED FULFILLMENT

This is another aspect of the mother's task in regard to needs. We have already looked at the ways in which pleasure-seeking and aggressive urges join forces with the need for nourishment and how the mother assists this process by making eating a pleasurable experience and by providing foods to chew, as soon as the child is ready. She also helps him channel anger into activity by allowing her infant to be an active participant in meeting his hunger need, through early self-feeding, and later through letting him help himself, take part in preparing and cooking foods, in choosing the menu, and so on. All this helps eating to be a good time, whereas lack of pleasurable feeding, lack of opportunity for chewing and for doing for himself, increases the child's anger, spoils his appetite, and reduces food to a necessary chore at best.

With sleep it works rather differently. Most people find it impossible to go full tilt, then simply lie down, turn off the light, and sleep. We usually need a transition period for doing things that help us get ready, to deal with tensions and "let down." We tend to slow down our activities, take care of our other needs so they won't get in the way (washing, toileting, having a bedtime snack or last drink of water), and we arrange our bedding in individual ways to be "comfy." We usually sleep best when our inner tensions are minimal, and may have trouble falling asleep or sleeping well when we are all "wound up," angry, and excited. Part of the process of getting ready for sleep thus includes satisfying our urges and reducing their claims. Children accomplish this by means of self-comforting activities, using different parts of their bodies at different levels of development, such as finger sucking, rocking, rubbing their cheeks, ears, navel, buttocks, and genital organs. As they come to know other calming satisfying activities, they may use them too, such as playing with their soft toys, singing or talking to themselves, daydreaming, or looking at books. All these practices help them discharge urges in preparation for sleeping, but they only serve well for coping with minor tensions. When the experiences of the day, and especially of the period prior to sleeping, have been very stimulating and have exacerbated the child's anger and excitement, his own means of discharge prove inadequate and sleep is interfered with. Parents usually know this. They help the child avoid excess stimulation, make the bedtime routines calm, and allow him a transition period of quiet undisturbed privacy in his bed so he can do his own relaxing before he is ready to sleep. Chasing around, wrestling, tickling, or angry altercations before bedtime are as notorious sleep interrupters as are the sounds of parental parties or arguments during the child's sleep period.

The need for elimination is spontaneously accompanied by urges, most strongly so during the child's second year when his voluntary sphincter muscles develop and enable him to exercise conscious control over urine and bowel movements. At this time both pleasure-seeking and aggressive urges are connected with expulsion and retention and with the body products themselves. Toddlers show great interest and satisfaction in the touch, smell, size, consistency, and even taste of their bodily products, and as many mothers learn, they also use them to express anger, to defy, to control, to withhold in protest, or to mess with.

With the help of these urges the children get to know and appreciate as their own, parts of the body which they cannot see or easily reach. In time, these urges also help toward independent toilet mastery. But their main contribution lies in being channeled and diverted into areas of activity. Mothers help by allowing the child to be active in achieving control and mastery of his toileting, and by offering and supporting substitute gratifications for his pleasures and anger. They let him "mess" with water and toys in the tub or sink; they let him "hoard" little treasures of stones, acorns, and other things he likes to pick up and hold onto; they encourage him to express anger in words and provide opportunity for energetic bodily movement and activity.

But in this area of the urges, as with independence, the road of development is not necessarily a smooth one. Mothers may err in not allowing enough instinctual gratification or in overstimulating the child's urges, or in not helping him to redirect and to gratify them in different forms. The child, in turn, may not be willing to give up his direct urge satisfactions and accept substitutions. The resulting interferences and conflicts show themselves in many different ways, often distorting the role of needs and need fulfillment. For example, some youngsters who are toilet trained in their first year by being put on the potty and have no later opportunity to expel or withhold their bowel movements at will make up for it in their eating habits. They may "hoard" their food in their cheeks instead of chewing and swallowing, and they may dawdle, smear, and mess excessively during meals. Or they may go to the opposite extreme and dread messiness so much that they don't want to feed themselves for fear of getting their hands dirty, and/or they may refuse all foods which vaguely remind them of stools in color or consistency, such as stews, puddings, boiled vegetables, or gravies.

But too much stimulation and gratification can also interfere: Tessa was not expected to become clean herself but her mother spent a lot of time cleaning her. For years she wiped and sponged Tessa's rectal and genital area, inspected it for rashes, powdered it and rubbed it with soothing ointments. Tessa liked these ministrations and invited them but could not cope with the excessive excitement they stimulated in her. She could not learn to master her toileting and kept on soiling, was always restless and irritable, with "ants in her pants" which prevented her from concentrating on play and activities in spite of good intelligence.

HELPING THE CHILD TO FIT NEED FULFILLMENT INTO DAILY LIVING

In the first few weeks, dealing with basic bodily needs makes up nearly all the business of the baby's daily life, but this soon changes. New needs arise, such as the need for company; urges manifest themselves more strongly and require their own gratifications, such as finger sucking; functions develop and have to be exercised, such as perception, motility, and speech. Increasingly, new activities, skills, and interests are learned and practiced. All this takes up time and energy, furnishes different satisfactions, and may conflict with the demands of the needs: "I am tired but I want to play longer"; "Running up and down the stairs is so much fun, I'll eat later." "Later" easily becomes "too late," when the overly hungry youngster greedily gulps down his food and gets a tummy ache, or when the overly tired one turns irritable and sleeps fitfully.

The fun of socializing with family members also starts to take up time and, increasingly, imposes conditions on the ways of meeting needs: "You can only sit at the dinner table with us if you eat nicely."; "You can't sit on Daddy's lap with dirty pants." In order to do all he wants to do and in order to be acceptable to all the people he wants to be with, the child has to learn to regulate his need fulfillments (for example, eat at certain times) and to attain satisfactions in a manner that is customary and expected within his family and community (for example, he needs to use a toilet for elimination).

It is no small achievement to keep our needs in proper perspective, to use "good manners" to satisfy them, and to live with them well. And it is, of course, the mother's job primarily to help her child achieve these difficult goals.

How does she go about it? And does the child work with her or against her? When it comes to regulating needs, the child works with her to a considerable extent. As his body grows bigger and stronger, needs become less frequent and urgent; for example, he eats more at one meal and gets hungry less often; he sleeps through the night and less during the day; and he can hold urine and stools for longer intervals and control elimination. The child's needs get used to daily rhythms and he can better tolerate and master their signals and postpone satisfactions. The mother watches for all these gradual changes and adjusts her expectations accordingly. She tries to keep to consistent meal and sleep times, gradually extends them to fit in with the family routines, and lets the child enjoy his new interests in between times. By and large this works out well for everyone. Sometimes it doesn't quite work out and there have to be makeshift arrangements; "The kids just can't wait when my husband gets home later, so I have to give them dinner earlier on those days"; "He didn't get his nap today because there was too much going on in the house, so he got crabby and I fed him early and let him go to bed early"; "When she's ill, she's off her schedule and nothing's right."

When families do not have routines, or when their routines are nowhere near the child's need rhythms (for example, very late dinners), the child cannot meet the expectations. He may get irritable and dissatisfied, may not be able to enjoy and enlarge his new interests and skills because his needs are never reliably at peace, and may, in the long run, have trouble regulating his needs and planning for and around them consistently. Many adults have trouble with this. Some don't get enough sleep, keep too busy, and endanger their health; some oversleep, get to work late, and endanger their jobs; some sleep at the wrong times, in the middle of a conversation, class, or at the movies. Likewise, some people never quite succeed in living well with their need for food, even when enough food is available to them. They may be unable ever to eat at a later hour or may forget about meals and then get terribly hungry; they may never remember to buy enough food and run out at inconvenient times or buy so much that it spoils before it can be used; they may regard eating as a necessary but unpleasant chore, or they may be so preoccupied with food that they have little time and energy to think of other things.

The younger the child, the better he thrives on "boring" routines, especially when it comes to need fulfillment. Variety only becomes the spice of life later, when the inner need signals are not so pressing and when need satisfaction is taken for granted and allows for some experimentation. Even as grown-ups, when we are ill, upset, or in a strange place, we often feel like a little child. We want our needs met at the right time and in the most familiar way because we worry a bit whether they will be met at all; for example, in the hospital nothing makes us more irritated than having to wait for our meal tray beyond the expected time, and there are few things we grumble about more than "How bad the food is." The dietitian just does not prepare our childhood favorites, and if she does, they don't quite taste the way we are used to, and, anyway, the nurse's aide may even forget to bring our food altogether! Similarly, on vacation trips, many people take no pleasure in getting to know differently equipped bedrooms and bathrooms and new tastes in foreign dishes, but distrust them on principle and search out places which meet their needs in familiar ways. That's one of the appeals of the Holiday Inn, McDonald's, and Kentucky Fried Chicken in such far-flung cities as Paris and Nairobi.

But when children who have experienced the reassuring routines of early need fulfillment get older, they seek out and enjoy the thrill of the new—new dishes, new ways of serving them, new kinds of bedding, and new bathrooms with different fixtures or even no fixtures, like in some campgrounds. Even at home they like to introduce changes: "Let's cook something different"; "Let's party through the night and not sleep at all"; or "Let's use sleeping bags in the living room or camp out in the backyard." And then it is often the parents who plump for the boring routines, half worried about their youngsters' health, half being set in their ways and dreading the extra work entailed.

When it comes to learning manners, the child also naturally meets the mother halfway in her attempts to teach him to satisfy his needs in the ways the adults do in the family, such as by sitting at the table, using implements for eating, waiting to be served, eating neatly, or keeping clean pants and using the toilet. Children who have a good enough relationship with their parents want to become like them and be appreciated by them. For this reason, they are, much of the time, eager to learn the parents' ways of satisfying needs, and parents usually appeal to their children on these lines: "Now you can use your fork like daddy" (or "Use the toilet like the grown-ups"); "You are getting so big. Isn't that nice. Aren't you proud of yourself." And when the child is not quite willing yet to make the extra effort, they encourage "*Soon* you'll want to eat nicely (or, stay clean) and *then* you'll be such a big boy/girl." They also point out the disadvantages of not having the right manners and therefore not being acceptable in "society." "You can't go to the restaurant with dirty pants, but when you get bigger and use the toilet and stay clean, then we can take you out for dinner."

Obviously, manners can only be acquired when the child becomes capable of developing the necessary inner controls and skills and when he wants to practice them with the help of his motivation: "I want to be big, I want to be like them." This implies that the adults set an example with their own manners, consistently. When manners are enforced before the child can manage them, they are so hard that they spoil the need satisfaction. Even grown-ups may say, "Using those chopsticks was so frustrating, I just couldn't enjoy the food and in the end gave up on it even though I was still hungry." Many of us also can only relish an orange, or watermelon, or piece of chicken, when we can hold it and bite into it, leaving aside all good manners.

When manners are required of the child but not of his loved adults, the child may perform well when watched but do without manners when he is not—in contrast to becoming a "gentleman" who, by one English definition, is "He who uses a butterknife when dining on his own." Toileting and sleeping also have to be performed with manners and there too the example of the adults in the family and the rules of the community matter. For example, the rule of privacy can only be learned when the adults in the family keep it. One little boy, reprimanded by his nursery school teacher for urinating in the playground, answered "My daddy does his wee-wee in the yard." His mother was quite embarrassed when she was informed and perhaps realized that it is hard for children to learn very different manners for home and school.

It is easy to see how often things can go awry in this area of the child's need education, how easily mother may expect too much or too little regulation and manners (expect perfect table manners of her four-year-old or let him feed himself with his hands); or may expect it too soon or too late (expect toilet mastery too soon or too late), or may expect her child to perform differently from Mom and Dad or differently at home and in public. It is equally easy to recognize that the child may, at one time, become angry because his dinner is not ready at the right time and, at another time, may become just as angry because he is not ready to eat it at the right time. He may refuse to use his home toilet at one time, and at a later time may refuse to use an unfamiliar toilet at the store. At best, the mother's correct gauging and the child's wish to become "big" will assure harmony most of the time, never all the time.

NEEDS AND THE MOTHER–CHILD RELATIONSHIP

Let us now turn to the mother–child relationship, the fulcrum through which the child's needs and their fulfillment are helped to take their rightful place in his life. Up until now we have looked at several aspects of the mothering person's task in regard to needs but we have hardly stressed that she does all she does as part of her close relationship with her child, and that this relationship is what makes it all work. Without this consistent, good enough relationship the mother could not feel with her child, could not sense what to do when, the child could not participate, respond, and make gains, and both of them could not feel good in the process (E. Furman, 1982a, 1994a).

The fortunate among us know that the crucial ingredient in a good meal is love (what else makes home cooking so special?), and that the snuggliest bed is made the way Mom or Dad used to tuck it in. Many of us also remember the joy of becoming independent, the pride in earning our first money and buying things with it. We may not recall the earliest steps along this road, the achievements of feeding and cleaning ourselves, and we rarely recognize that wanting to do for ourselves and enjoying it only happens to those of us who have had a full, loved, and loving share of being cared for and of having received support and admiration for wanting to be independent.

The mutually loving mother–child relationship adds a mutually satisfying element to need fulfillment, an important way of being together and doing together. It is no accident that "feeder" means both the one who provides the food and the one who eats it. During the first months the mother–child unit is so close that they almost perceive the two functions as one. Later, when they love each other as more separate people, eating together still makes up much of the fun of eating, and even adults usually prefer company at meals to eating alone. Eating alone does not taste so good.

That's why some of us can't be bothered to fix a meal for ourselves, and others overeat when alone, in the vain hope that more food can make up for the love of another. But in many areas of need fulfillment, doing for oneself does not mean missing out. With toileting, dressing, even sleeping, the first steps toward independence still include mother in a new social role, that of supporter and admirer. In time, children take all these forms of mother's love into themselves and, in caring for themselves, love themselves as she loved them (E. Furman, 1992, 1993).

The "it's fun doing it together" social aspect, which the mother–child relationship imparts to need fulfillment, is in part related to the urges. As we have said before, the pleasure-seeking urges are experienced in many body parts, most of which are also connected with needs and need fulfillment. To some extent they are gratified by the child's own activities: Mouthing, eating, chewing, and thumb sucking gratify the mouth. But this leaves out the most important aspect of the urges, the fact that, almost from the start, they are focused on a loved person. They are stimulated and gratified through the bodily and social interaction with this loved person, as well as channeled and modified through the mutual bond. The mothering person is the young child's main loved one, and the child is one of the main loved ones to her. Her ministrations of suckling, feeding, holding, cleansing, and rocking stimulate and gratify primitive bodily sexual feelings and her ongoing relationship with the child helps to develop the subtler feelings of fondness and affection, of caring and sharing and being together. The child, in turn, stimulates and gratifies the mother. Mothers often experience nursing, fondling, kissing, and holding their baby as exciting and gratifying. At the same time, this fosters their fondness for the child and their enjoyment of his demonstrative love and closeness. This bodily and mental bond, forged in part with the help of the pleasure-seeking urges, makes the child as indispensable to the mother as she is to him. Through this relationship, the mother not only furthers the child's enjoyment of need fulfillment but, in Freud's words, teaches her child how to love. The need oriented pleasures of the early mother–child relationship lay the groundwork for the much later, very sophisticated pattern of adult family life. Within its framework the erstwhile youngster will, once again, combine all these trends: the bonds of consistent caring fondness and affection with a sexual partner, the enjoyment of meeting his own and each other's needs, and the ability to include children in this partnership and to do the same for them. But all this is a long way off in the distant future and does not preoccupy mother or child as they go about the business of enjoying need fulfillment with each other.

One of the things that sometimes *is* on their minds is the fact that there is not only love and fun in their relationship. The mother is also the first main object of the child's aggressive urges, the target for his anger. He initially attacks her directly, biting, pushing, hitting, and pinching, and learns only gradually, through the relationship with her, how to express and channel his anger so as not to harm her. The mother's anger at the child is inevitable too, but it is, one hopes, already mitigated by her love and well controlled and modified in its expression. For this reason she does not harm him and helps him to cope with his anger. When there is not too much anger in the relationship, it can be accommodated, partly expressed in words, partly channeled and modified. Most of the time, even the mother's gradual attempts at regulating the child's needs and teaching of manners do not arouse too much anger in the child, just as she does not become too angry when he resists her lead, does not always meet her expectations, or protests against them as an annoying interference. After all, this too is tempered by the helpful aspects of the relationship, the wish to become like the loved parents and to be appreciated by them.

When all goes well, the mother–child relationship works for the best and manages to interweave all the various strands into the solid fabric of personality growth for the child along with pleasure and satisfaction for him and his parents. Perhaps the most amazing thing is that, thanks to their relationship with the child, mothers don't have to reason out all the steps in their difficult task but can rely on their loving "feel" to get it right and to adjust it when it isn't quite right. But to build this kind of relationship which can coordinate and balance so many diverse forces within it takes real, loving investment and a lot of devoted time and energy. Without that it cannot do its work and cannot bring sufficient pleasure to mother or child, to make up for the inevitable moments of mutual hardship and frustration.

Mother–child relationships are never ideal, only good enough at best. They are subject to many strains and stresses and when something goes awry, it often shows up as an interference in the mother–child interactions around need fulfillment and in the child's attitude to his needs. The numerous eating, sleeping, and toileting problems of young children indicate just how frequently such difficulties arise, and mothers' equally frequent puzzlement, annoyance, unhappiness, and guilt over them shows just how much they experience them as an obstacle in the relationship with the child and, often as not, as a failure on their part.

Some of the difficulties may indeed be due to the mother, others may be due to the child, and yet others may be due to extraneous events which impinge on their relationship, such as illness. Often enough, these factors combine and reinforce each other. Sometimes even the happiest family events, such as the birth of a new baby, may unbalance the mother–child relationship and affect their interactions around need fulfillment. For example, it is not uncommon for youngsters to react to the arrival of a sibling with sleep difficulties and loss of independence in self-feeding and toileting.

Sometimes difficulties with need fulfillment are not caused by disharmonies in the mother–child relationship but stem from the relationship itself. This happens when need fulfillment mainly serves to make the relationship gratifying, instead of the relationship serving to make need fulfillment gratifying: For example, eating and feeding can become a main way of showing love, instead of love adding to the pleasure of eating. With young children this happens very readily because they connect their feelings about mother so intimately with their own needs that they often fail to distinguish who really is gratified when their needs are met. They may eat when they like mother and want to please her, but grumble about her food or even refuse it when they are angry at her. Likewise, they may go to sleep nicely and produce their bowel movements in the toilet as though it were a loving gift for mother, rather than a satisfaction for themselves. Wise mothers sense this and do their utmost to set things straight for the child, in their attitude, behavior, and words. For example, when the child enjoys his dinner, the mother does not congratulate herself and take it as a proof of the child's love but stresses that *he* had himself a good time eating and she is glad for him; and when he is fussy, doesn't like what she cooked, and doesn't finish his meal, she doesn't feel rejected and hurt but says she's sorry he couldn't enjoy it and will perhaps feel more hungry tomorrow. The child's appetite, sleep, or stools are neither a reward nor an insult to *her.* If she has reason to suspect that the child's behavior is prompted by anger at her, she may even say, "It looks like you're angry at me. You could tell me what it is about. When you don't eat (or dirty your pants) you are mean to yourself, not to me. You can be mad at me and still enjoy your dinner (or be a big boy with clean pants)."

Even the wisest mothers, however, are not always wise. Their necessary closeness with their young child tends to make them feel and think as he does. As a result, they too may confuse who really benefits when the child eats well ("He won't eat *for me*") and who is disgraced when he is soiled ("*We* had three pairs of dirty pants today. I just don't know what to do!"). At such times it helps mothers to remind themselves that needs are ultimately every person's, even the youngest child's, own business (E. Furman, 1982a, 1992, 1993, 1994a).

WOULD IT NOT HELP IF OTHERS, LIKE THE FATHER, TOOK OVER SOME OF THE CHILD'S NEED FULFILLMENT?

The mother–child relationship, in our context, means the relationship with the mothering person, who usually but not always, is the mother. Her place in the primary one-to-one relationship may be taken by someone else, such as the father or grandmother. The primary relationship itself, however, is essential for the child's physical and mental survival during the first one to two years. Need fulfillment is inevitably a part of this relationship and the foundations of the child's attitudes to his needs are laid during this first period. By the time a child is two-and-a-half to three years old, he has usually taken over much of his bodily self-care (self-feeding with implements, toilet mastery, sleeping on his own, avoiding common dangers, the basic parts of washing and dressing himself). Beyond these early years, and with the basics accomplished, the child's need education continues and both parents contribute to it in varying measure, depending on the customs of the individual family. During the earlier period, there are usually times when mother-substitutes (father, grandmother, sitter) help out. Up to a point this works out well for all, and the child's growing relationships with the father and other family members help him to be interested in things other than need fulfillment which helps to put it in perspective.

However, when the mothering person shares with others too many of her need fulfilling interactions too often during the early period, it does not help. The shared need fulfilling times are important to the maintenance of the relationship, to the mother's ability to remain in tune with her infant, to the child's ability to love her and respond to her, and to the special pleasures each derives from them. When the primary relationship becomes too diluted, it becomes burdened with excessive anger or even indifference and can't do its essential beneficial work (R. A. Furman, 1983; E. Furman, 1984a).

The one-to-one early relationship does have its drawbacks, but we can't cure them by throwing out the baby with the bath water. A more effective cure to the entanglements of the relationship are (1) for the mother to be aware of the pitfalls; (2) for the child to take over his own need fulfillment which he usually wants to do sooner when he has had good one-to-one care; and (3) for needs to be met only when they have had a chance to assert themselves, such as offering food only when the child is really hungry, expecting him to sleep when he is really tired. This helps to foster the child's self-reliance and prevents need fulfillment from unnecessary and prolonged entanglement with the mother–child relationship.

WHEN SHOULD CHILDREN START TOILETING? SHOULD CHILDREN HAVE TO TASTE EVERY DISH? SHOULD CHILDREN EVER BE ALLOWED TO STAY UP LATE?

It does not usually help to hand out specific "prescriptions" for these and other queries. What to do in a certain situation depends on the child, the parents, the family's current and past experiences. The "right" thing for one mother and child may be "wrong" for another. Advice therefore always requires a very good understanding of all the many factors at play. And it works best when the parents and child are able to listen and respond to each other, to gauge what fits, and to correct what doesn't. Even the "right" measure can turn out to be "wrong" in a relationship which lacks trust and mutual respect.

WHEN SHOULD PARENTS GET PROFESSIONAL HELP WITH THEIR CHILD'S DIFFICULTIES AROUND NEEDS?

In two situations: (1) When they are concerned. To an outsider the child's difficulty may appear negligible, but the parents' concern always implies that they sense something that deserves being looked into. (2) When the child's need fulfillment and need education is interfered with over a period of time: when he cannot enjoy need fulfillment, such as by experiencing loss of appetite, sleep troubles; when he cannot, age appropriately, take over responsibility for self-care, can't achieve toilet mastery, is persistently unwilling to learn to dress and wash himself; or when he cannot learn to regulate his needs age-appropriately; for example, falls asleep at school, always needs to go to the bathroom during class.

DO CHILDREN OUTGROW THEIR DIFFICULTIES WITH NEEDS?

It depends on the difficulty and on its causes. For example, a child's poor appetite may be due to the fact that he is expected to eat more than his hunger warrants. This may correct itself when he has a growth spurt, when he becomes bodily more active, or when he is allowed to help himself. However, a child's poor appetite may be due to not enjoying eating, perhaps because he is at a day care center and misses his mom (in which case his difficulty may subside when he is helped to overcome the stress or when he has a chance to eat more with Mom during home meals). It may be due to an early difficulty in experiencing feeding as pleasurable (in which case his lack of appetite is not so likely to subside and, depending on the extent of the trouble, may endanger his health at a later time or may just mean that eating will never be important to him).

Development does tend to affect our attitudes to needs. During the elementary school years, the parent–child relationship is less intimate and need fulfillment naturally becomes more the child's own affair. In the process it usually sheds some of the earlier "for or against the parents" interferences. In adolescence, the newly powerful urges usually "invade" needs (eating binges and diets alternate, as do sleeping late and going without sleep, spending hours on bodily cleanliness and neglecting to wash his clothes or clean his room). During late adolescence and early adulthood, new identifications with the parents and others again help to reshape our attitudes to needs. But all these progressive changes rest on the early foundation and don't stray too far from it, for better or worse.

3
Pleasure in Living

When we enjoy many things in life very much, we feel good and living always seems worthwhile. We can even take in stride the inevitable hardships and make up for the loss of some pleasures because we have others left to choose from. When we enjoy only very few things very seldom, we feel unhappy and living does not seem so worthwhile. Every upset looms large and adds to our burden of misery, and when we are deprived of our few ways of having fun we have nothing to put in their place. For life to continue at all, there has to be some pleasure in living and that is the business of the pleasure-seeking urges. Fortunately, they are so flexible that, with the help of maturation and environment, they can come to be gratified in the most varied ways, in keeping with the kinds of pleasure particular societies and individuals permit and value.

Guiding the pleasure-seeking urges is largely the task of the parents during the child's years of emotional growth. It is an especially intricate task because the parents are not outsiders to the child's urges. As we have already seen, they are also participants in their child's pleasures, they stimulate and gratify them, and they experience pleasure themselves in doing so. Yet without this kind of relationship they cannot help their child to feel good, to modify and divert his satisfactions, and to find new ways of gaining pleasure.

BACKGROUND ABOUT THE
PLEASURE-SEEKING URGES

In *Relationships in Early Childhood* (E. Furman, 1998a) and *Self-Control and Mastery in Early Childhood* (E. Furman, 1998b), we discussed a number of ways in which the pleasure-seeking urges work within the child's growing personality, and how the parents use and guide them through their relationship with the child. Let us summarize them here. These urges contribute to the enjoyment of need fulfillment, serving self-preservation (eating, eliminating, sleeping, liking his body and protecting it from harm).

In following the development of personality functions (tools of mastery) (E. Furman, 1998b), we observed how, with the help of the parents' pleasure and appreciation, these urges are channeled into motility, speech, perception, and thinking. For example, in watching the toddler's ecstatic joy in running around, in crawling under and out of furniture, in pushing chairs and toys, and his thrill in babbling and forming words, we could feel with him his initial intense excitement in exercising his new abilities. In the course of development, they cease to be an end in themselves and come to serve him as tools for achieving other goals. In the process, the early excited delight is toned down to a more subtle sense of well-being, so much so that, as adults, we are hardly aware of it unless illness or unusual circumstances prevent us from using these functions. Then, and only then, do we realize what we have lost and can perhaps reexperience the infantile intense pleasure when we can resume walking or talking.

We have also observed how pleasure fuels the beginnings of the mother–child relationship in the first year (E. Furman, 1998a). The pleasure-seeking urges are stimulated and gratified in the daily bodily interactions between mother and child around need fulfillment and affectionate interplays and are gradually toned down to mental feelings of loving, fondness, liking, and caring. The pleasurable experiences of this first relationship prompt the child to seek out new relationships with the father and others in the family, and in the wider community, until ultimately they contribute to his or her adult relationships, sexual and non-sexual.

In *Self-Control and Mastery in Early Childhood* we have noted that the pleasures derived from the early relationships with the parents are so great and so important that, for the sake of preserving them, the child is willing to take disappointments in stride and to learn to tolerate frustrations, to curb some of his satisfactions ("You have to eat with your spoon, not with your fingers") and to forego others ("No, you can't mess with your BMs"), and to take the parental love and demands into himself and make them a permanent part of his own personality in the form of self-esteem and conscience.

But we have also seen that, from early on, the child gratifies some of his bodily pleasure-seeking urges himself and that this helps him to be less dependent on the parents; for example, when the baby sucks his thumb or fingers, he provides pleasure and comfort for himself. We mentioned that the child's self-comforting activities tend to be focused on those parts of the body which, at successive stages in his development, are the main source of pleasurable feelings for him—the mouth in infancy, the rectal area during toddlerhood, and the genitals from the preschool years on—keeping in mind that there is also much overlap between these phases and that, all along, other body parts also provide pleasure. Among these are various body hollows (ears, nose, navel), the skin (providing pleasure in bathing, cleansing, caressing, holding), postural and muscle sensations stimulated through passive movement (rocking, swinging, being driven in a car), and through active movement (kicking, throwing, pushing, running, pedaling a tricycle, or using a swing). Many young children rub their cheeks, play with their fingers in their ears or noses, rock themselves as they go to sleep or on a rocking horse, jump up and down on beds, or seemingly never tire of swinging on a swing.

We have also already looked more closely at the role some of these infantile pleasure zones play in the child's later personality, and have followed the pathways by which they contribute to his growth and well-being. In regard to the early mouth pleasures we traced their later direct manifestations (enjoying eating, kissing as a way of showing affection, and as a part of adult sexual foreplay), their contribution in modified form (enjoyment of talking and singing), and their part in nonbodily mental activity (the enjoyment of "taking in" information, attitudes, and ideals and the important part this plays in learning and in acquiring personality traits and values).

Last but not least, we have touched on some of the conflicts the pleasure-seeking urges may cause, especially when they are gratified too little or too much; for example, the child may not want to give up mother's pleasurable care of his body, or may insist on pursuing his own pleasures independently of her.

THE CHANGING PATTERNS OF PLEASURES

As the child develops, some new pleasures emerge naturally on their own. Maturation itself transforms the needy greedy baby with his mouth-centered excitements and satisfactions into the assertive toddler who likes to be his own boss and do his own thing in his own way. He even wants to be boss of his mother, hugging, clinging, teasing, and tormenting her with his "yes–no" love, engaging her in tussles of tug-of-war, shrieking with delight as he runs away from her and invites her to chase after him, and clashing with her over their different ideas of what is fun. Depending on the mothers' attitude, and perhaps on just how pleased or exasperated they feel at the moment, they may describe their toddler as "He is so positive these days" or "She is so negative." Some of the child's new pleasures are readily shared by the mother, at least much of the time: the pleasures in motility, in talking, and in independent mastery, the pervasive "Me all by myself" when it comes to doing anything at all. In regard to other pleasures there is much divergence between them: The toddler likes to take apart, destroy, and throw away many of the things the mother treasures, but likes to hoard and collect many of the things she wants to get rid of. He "attacks" indiscriminately her pots, pans, and knick-knacks as well as his own new toys, and even when he asks her to make sandpies or build block towers, his main fun comes in knocking them down gleefully. At the same time he fills his hands, pockets, and even mouth with stones, acorns, buttons, and beads and, to her dismay, hoards little caches of such "valuables." He likes to mess with things, while she prefers to keep them neat and clean and responds with disgust or annoyance when she finds him, once again, joyfully scattering the contents of drawers, smearing food on himself and his high chair, or splashing water from the faucet. Their clash over pleasures is especially pronounced when it comes to his favorite absorbing interest, the urine and bowel movements produced by himself and others. On a walk the toddler notices every dog turd. On the visit to the farm or zoo, his highlights are the defecating and urinating animals. Who did it, how big is it, how does it smell, and can one touch it and pick it up are a never ending source of comments and questions. And this applies most especially to his own productions. We see it in the child's intensely preoccupied expression when he "makes" or holds back, squirming and wriggling, in his fascinated inspection of the contents of diapers and toilets, often accompanied by attempts to stir them around and examine them, in his delighted comparison of their size and consistency. Not only mothers, but fathers and baby-sitters are often called to admire "See, two big ones!" The child's pleasure even extends to the idea of tasting bodily products, as illustrated by one verbally precocious fourteen-month-old. During a contented family meal of hot dogs she suddenly pointed to the mustard jar and asked "Please pass the BM." Her parents sat stunned into silence and only her four-year-old sister remained unruffled and fulfilled the request with the simple comment, "It's mustard. We don't eat BM."

In time the toddler pleasures subside and are, again spontaneously, overshadowed by the new pleasures of the nursery years. The parents welcome them with mixed feelings. On one hand they are glad that their child now maintains a more cooperative relationship with both of them, enjoys following the lead of their interests, and wants to do what they do, be it cooking, shopping, or working in the yard. They are flattered by his admiration of them and proud of his inquisitiveness, gladly demonstrate their skills, encourage his efforts to help and learn, and patiently answer his many questions of why and how. They also fulfill quite happily their other role in the "mutual admiration society" with their child, respond to his constant demands of "Look at me," "See what I can do" with duly complimentary interest, and share his great pleasure in achieving "superior status," be it a new skill in drawing a picture or looking impressively handsome in a new outfit, or looming extra tall from the top of the jungle gym. On the other hand, they often view with some misgivings the fact that their youngster's curiosity and pleasure in showing off tends to focus on bodily, especially sexual, attributes. Not only has their interest in animals shifted to checking which are "Mommies" and "Daddies" and "Baby" dogs (cats, elephants, or horses), comparing the sizes, presence or absence of penises, and taking a keen interest in everything they do with them and with each other, but boys and girls show even greater fascination with exploring all this in people. They ask personal questions of family members, teachers, and sometimes strangers. They want to look at and know all about the different sexual organs and functions in men and women, boys and girls, and of course in their own bodies.

Being looked at is as much fun for them as looking. They often use any opportunity or pretext to prance around in the nude, like to run around naked at dressing and undressing times, and are apt to appear bare of an evening in the living room, just when neighbors have stopped over, with a righteous "Mommy, I can't find my nightie." One youngster even threw off his clothes, danced in the driveway and, when his surprised Mom came upon him, greeted her with "Spring has come!" More subtly, they tend to lift their dresses or don't quite finish pulling up their pants before leaving the bathroom. They also like to show off in words, sometimes in unexpected ways; for example, four-year-old Harry boasted to his nursery school class "My daddy has the biggest penis in the whole town."

Doing and wanting to do go with the pleasure in mutual looking. Youngsters may touch and handle their genitals, squeeze their thighs together, or hold back urine to experience and experiment with the many pleasurable sensations in this bodily area. They become easily stimulated and excited by bodily interactions with others: "Mommy, I want *you* to dry me. It tickles so nicely"; "Daddy, swing me around again and again." They may like to bump up and down on Dad's knees or hang around his neck, touch the front of Mommy's blouse or push into her. Shared toileting, bathing, and sleeping as well as playing "family" and "doctor" with siblings or peers readily turn into mutual excited exploring and touching. The young child's own feelings also make him aware of the parents' adult intimate relationship and he wants to share in that too. Boys and girls often want to sleep in the parents' bed or have one parent sleep with them. They interrupt parents kissing, or even parents talking together. They imitate the parents' affectionate gestures with one another and try to treat the parent as their partner; for example, Paul would give his mother's behind a pat and put his arm round her as he had seen his father do. Valerie asked her dad, "Dance close with me, like you do with mommy," and offers of "I'll marry you mommy (or daddy)" are frequent (E. Furman, 1985, 1998a).

These infantile, pleasure-seeking urges wax and wane as they succeed each other and pave the way for the beginnings of adult sexuality in adolescence. Some of them become a part of personal well-being (for example, feeling good about one's genitals), others contribute elements to later sexual enjoyment but will need to be directed to new loved ones outside the family (for example, wishing for a sexual partner and including looking and being looked at in sexual foreplay). Some of these urges are unhelpful in their original form (for example, the pleasure in messing, in destroying, tormenting, teasing, and being contrary). All of them, however, can contribute in an important way to the growth and enrichment of the child's personality if their energy is channeled into new pathways and gratified in new forms.

GETTING TO KNOW NEW PLEASURES

Children who have enjoyed life are usually eager to experience any new pleasure, especially when their trusted loved ones offer it, when they see them enjoy it, are drawn by the prospect of sharing it with them, and becoming like them. If Mom or Dad enjoy mixing the dough for cookies, washing the car, building sand castles, drawing, reading, tidying up, or whatever, surely it must be fun, and surely it must be fun to do it with them and like them: "Let me! I want to too!" But children often find that the new "funs" are not so easy to come by and involve some sacrifices. They usually entail skills that have to be learned, effort has to be put into the process, frustrating hurdles overcome, and restrictions observed; for example, "You can help me mix the dough, but—you have to put on an apron, you mustn't lick your fingers, it mustn't get on the floor, it has to be done this way and not that way, and no, you can't suddenly leave it and do something else without getting cleaned up." All this diminishes the fun of doing, delays the pleasure in the final accomplishment, and, even when one has mastered it all in the end, the new pleasure feels very different from the old one. Mixing dough well for real cookies is fun but not easy fun like "just messing" or making mudpies, and it is indeed far removed from it, in spite of some similarities. The old fun is all body pleasure, immediate and intense. The new fun is largely mental, subtler, toned down, slower to achieve. New pleasures, like all acquired tastes, take time and repeated experience before we can really enjoy them and appreciate their greatest advantage, the glow of the aftertaste. This part was altogether absent in the old pleasures whose fun stopped the moment we finished doing. The new pleasures last. They leave us feeling good and proud of ourselves long after the activity has ceased, and they earn appreciation from those whose opinions matter. These are powerful enticements to try again, to savor ever more new pleasures, to perfect mastery, and to add self-esteem combined with praise (E. Furman, 1994b).

Learning new pleasures always entails some giving up of the old ones. They are mostly offered, not in addition, but instead; that is their other drawback. They come in parental terms of not this but that, not here but there, and sometimes of not now but later. "You can play with dough but not with mud (and certainly not with bowel movements)," "You can be naked in private but not in public," "You can't have a husband or wife now but only when you grow up" (which seems an eternity away). In some instances, new pleasures even involve a complete turn around: "You mustn't enjoy being messy, you need to enjoy being clean" or "You mustn't enjoy

being cruel, you have to enjoy showing pity and being kind."
This expectation of giving up the infantile body pleasures
becomes obvious from the way parents prohibit or discour-
age them, and from the way they interfere with the new pleasures as soon as the child shows signs of changing them back
into his old ones; for example, when mixing dough deterio-
rates into real messing, Mom or Dad stop it: "That's not for
messing. That's for making cookies. If you can't yet do that
properly and go by the rules, we'll have to wait till you get
bigger but you'll have to stop for now." All this giving up and
trying is hard enough in the many situations where the child's
efforts are rewarded by joining the parents in their fun and
doing as they do. It is harder yet when he has to renounce
enjoyments they can pursue (such as when the child is not
allowed to gratify his wish for bodily intimacy with the parents, but they can do so with each other). It is also hard when
the activities they enjoy are still beyond his capacities—
bodily ones, like making babies, and nonbodily ones, like
reading, writing, driving a car, cooking a meal. One young
woman recalled, during a class discussion of this topic, her
envious admiration of her mother writing checks, how des-
perately she scribbled on little pieces of paper to produce
her own "checks," and how relieved she was when her
mother, instead of laughing at her, said kindly "You'll learn.
Your time will come" (E. Furman, 1992, 1993).

Obviously, channeling and transforming urges is not
quick and easy. It often goes back and forth. In nursery school
many children already use paints well, put the brushes in
the jars with the appropriate color, apply paint only to the
paper, and try to produce a picture with form and even content. But even an accomplished young painter who really
enjoys painting and is pleased and proud with his finished
product is apt to have days when he, once again, indulges in
messing. Then the paints drip on the floor and make a gooey
scribble on the paper; his hands get painted or his clothes;
and, unless a watchful teacher intervenes, the whole enter-
prise can quickly turn into a gleeful orgy of splattering paints
on others and on the furniture. Nursery teachers have to be
very watchful, and are well aware that their pupils still travel
the rocky road toward new pleasures. Parents have known it

long before their children even enter nursery school. They know how to gauge when the child is ready to give up a pleasure (usually when he has developed enough skills to be somewhat successful at new pleasures); they know which new pleasure to offer and how to make the transition gradual (for example, they start with water play and work up, step by step, toward paint with brushes); they know how to encourage and praise every move in the right direction and to help overcome failures and setbacks ("*Soon* you'll know how").

Above all, parents use words and support the child in using words to name and express his feelings, wishes, and thoughts. We already know how this helps. It provides a means of mastery and an avenue for limited discharge and gratification. We use words as a tool for thinking, for expressing and communicating *instead* of doing, and this makes it possible to have and enjoy the feelings, and yet control our behavior. In our society's laws this is recognized in the freedom of thought and speech. Privately, for the child, and later for the adult, it means that we can think what we want, that we can, more or less, say what we want, and that we can pretend, that is, fulfill our wishes in daydreams and, to some extent, in play. All these are satisfying outlets. They are not as satisfying as real doing but satisfying enough to bear the frustration of not doing. The child's emphatic "But I don't want to sleep in my bed. I want to sleep with you" helps him to conform to his parents' expectation of "I can understand that you want to and you can say it, but you can't really do it. I know it's hard, but you need to sleep in your bed and you'll be okay." Alone in his bed, many a child daydreams that he is sleeping with the parents after all, and when he plays "house" with his friends at nursery school he may take the pretend role of daddy and assign a place for his pretend bedroom with the pretend mommy. Without words all this limited and harmless fun would be denied to him. He would find it much harder to give up his infantile pleasures and to invest his energy in the new ones (Katan, 1961).

Words are especially helpful to the child and parents in coping with the early interests in and feelings about sexual organs and functions. In this area the parents cannot directly participate in the child's pleasures. Opportunities for looking further stimulate youngsters' urges and, at the same time, fail to convey accurate information. Going by what they can see, children can't help but arrive at the erroneous conclusion that boys are "haves" and girls "have-nots" because the crucial internal differences are not visible. And moreover adults of their own sex seem totally different because the secondary sexual characteristics obscure the similarities between the child's and adult's body. However, when parents respond to the child's interest by sharing truthful knowledge in simple, not technical, words, they satisfy his curiosity sufficiently, without adding to his excitement and without fully excluding him. Knowing about sexual matters through words also helps children feel good about their sexual identity and future sexual role, and enables them to renounce their sexual demands on the parents in favor of nonsexual bonds of caring and affection. Not least, it assists in diverting their curiosity to learning about other things. As such it becomes an important part of self-motivated learning and finding out about the world (E. Furman, 1985).

WHAT ARE THE NEW PLEASURES AND HOW DO THEY ENRICH THE PERSONALITY?

Each infantile pleasure follows its own new channels. Some we have already discussed. For example, we saw that some of the child's love of messing is allowed substitute satisfaction with water, sand, clay, and can gradually lead to a new nonbodily pleasure in art and craft. Paint, a potentially messy medium, gets to be used to produce pictures or to paint houses, walls, and furniture. Liking to "get one's hands into it" becomes a part of gardening, cleaning, and cooking (how else can one make a meatloaf?). The young child's pleasure in possessing and hoarding can become more discriminate and lead to valuing and caring for his clothes, toys, money, artwork, and other skilled productions, as well as to enjoyable hobbies, or even professions, of collecting (trading cards, stamps, coins, books, art objects, antiques). The early pleasure in being the boss of his stools and urine contributes not only to toilet mastery but to the pleasure in all masteries. It plays an important part in overcoming obstacles to achievement, in persevering with activities, and in enjoying accomplishments, a good job well done.

We have also already spoken of the way the child's infantile sexual curiosity finds new nonsexual gratifications in intellectual curiosity and in learning. The fun of being looked at, of showing off his body, is, with parental help, channeled into showing off clothes ("What a pretty dress!") and, more importantly, skills and achievements. Most preschoolers show off everything they do and make to their teacher, then keep it to show the parents and solicit their admiration, and like to put it up for display. Many refrigerators, bulletin boards, doors, shelves, and walls blossom with the children's productions, a constant source of pride to them and testimony to the parents' shared pleasure and efforts at supporting his development. Once showing off relinquishes its primitive exciting quality, it is used in feeling good about performing in front of others, be it reading aloud to the class, acting in a play, giving a talk, or just speaking up in discussions. Even the young child's wish to make a baby like the parents is partially diverted into the pleasure of creativity. It may be a humble little project, a special way of decorating the table or of arranging flowers, a newly invented game, a magic trick, a scientific theory, a work of art. It is always a special thrill to create something new. We acknowledge the early connection when we speak of "my brainchild" or "the father of the idea."

But what about those early pleasures which are mostly unhelpful in later life and need to be turned around? How does the child who likes himself dirty come to like himself clean, and how does his enjoyment of hurting change to wanting to feel pity? Mothers often puzzle about that too. Some despair of ever getting their toddlers to be clean, much less wanting to be clean, while others say, "Why, I didn't do anything at all. He just trained himself." They overlook the fact that the child's wanting to be clean is not a question of training or not training, but of helping the child to be master of himself, and that a crucial element in this process is the child's changing attitude to dirt. That which was enjoyed turns into a source of disgust, and liking himself clean becomes the new pleasure. This is not accomplished by putting, or not putting, the child on the potty, by guessing when he needs to eliminate or by disregarding it. It happens gradually and inconspicuously through the mother–child relationship. In the beginning, especially when the baby is breast-fed and mother's milk makes up his main food intake, his stools are such that mothers, as a rule, do not mind taking care of them. But as new foods are added and increasingly outweigh or supplant nursing, the child's stools change and so does the mother's response. Thus, from the end of his first year on, when infants watch their mother's face as she changes their diapers, disposes of the contents, and cleanses their bodies, they invariably see an expression of involuntary disgust, at least a slightly wrinkled nose. They may also hear her comments to that effect, notice some fastidiousness in her movements when she, perhaps gingerly, handles the dirty items. And when she is done, or almost done, Mother usually shows relief, may smile, hug her child, and say something about how nice he now smells and how good he looks to her when he is all clean. Most mothers are quite unaware of all this, but the child "drinks it in." Sometimes he imitates her: We often see very young toddlers with a disgusted face or repeating little phrases and exclamations of disgust ("Pooh, yucky!") while they happily stick their hands into the diaper pail or unflushed toilet. Their new disgust is wafer thin, no patch yet on the real pleasure in messing, but it may be a first sign of inner struggle between the two different attitudes. Later, teddy bears are sometimes told with disgust that they are dirty and smelly, although the child still does not object to this in himself. But in time this changes with the impact of the parents' attitude—their direct or indirect disgust at bodily products, their enjoyment of being clean themselves, their spontaneous closeness with the child when he is clean, their expectation and trust that he can become clean like them, and the child's admiration of them and wish to grow up. When children first repudiate dirtiness, and make being clean their own thing, they often overshoot. They don't want to eat foods that remind them of bodily products, they may become fiends at cleaning up everything, or lining up everyone's shoes, they may not even want to go in the water, having just decided that it was "yucky" to be wet. All of this usually subsides in time and tones down to a reasonable pleasure in keeping themselves, their possessions, and surroundings neat and clean (R. A. Furman, 1991).

Likewise, the relationship with the parents and the example they set helps to reverse the child's enjoyment of hurting into becoming compassionate. The parents show their attitude in many ways: in their response to the child when he is hurt ("I am so sorry."; "Poor thing."; "There, there."; "Let me help make it better."), in their compassion for other people and indeed for all living things, in their avoidance of inflicting pain on the child and others, and in their preventing or stopping the child from hurting anyone. How often children gleefully step on worms or ants, tease the dog or cat or their siblings, and how often parents swiftly interfere "Oh, no! That's not kind! Poor little thing. Come and be nice." Sometimes the pleasure in hurting is enjoyed vicariously, as in a morbid eagerness to hear of misfortunes, tragedies, and violence, or in watching, with fascination, movies and real incidents where people and animals are hurt, or in laughing when someone gets hurt. Young children's pleasure in hurting is unduly stimulated in such situations. They do not serve as a helpful outlet. Since in our Western societies cruelty is increasingly not permitted, a child's well-developed aversion to it and capacity for feeling pity will stand him in good stead in life. It will also help him to avoid developing a pleasure in being hurt, which is often the natural companion of hurting and which, if stimulated, may persist and interfere with his well-being. This is also one of the reasons against the use of physical punishment (E. Furman, 1982b, 1992, 1993, 1998b).

TWO STEPS FORWARD AND ONE BACK

Development never proceeds in a smooth, direct line. The process of growing up, and changing urge satisfactions is a part of it, tends to grind to a temporary halt from time to time, and to go back and forth. Sometimes this is caused by the stress of an illness, of a change in routines, of family upheaval, or even of fatigue at the end of a long day. Sometimes the effort of coping with new maturational challenges is just too great to be sustained and progress takes a bit of "time out." As long as the child can recoup and resume the forward momentum, as long as he takes the proverbial two steps forward and one back in an ongoing way, he is doing all right. Parents and educators often have a hard time realizing this. They get so frustrated and worried, fearing that the child will get stuck and never make it, that they even forget that the child feels the same way, disappointed, hopeless, upset, and angry. The child is apt to feel even worse than the adults because he has not yet had the experience of being grown-up, of making it. For him the distance looms so great, the goals seem so unattainable. It helps a lot when the parents put the setbacks in perspective and convey their trust that things will go better again, and encourage the child along the way: "It's hard now but that happens to everyone. Soon things will go better. Just keep trying."

The parents' concern, however, is not always unfounded. Children can get "stuck" at a particular level and they can take steps back which are not followed by steps forward. How does one know when this has happened, and what causes it? Parents usually know that development is interfered with when the child reaches the next phase in age but not in appropriate functioning; for example, he or she may get to be a preschooler but continues to act like a toddler, or reverts to toddlerlike behavior for a long period, may mess instead of being pleased to keep clean, may enjoy teasing and being contrary instead of taking pleasure in showing up well. Similarly, a school-aged child may act like a preschooler or even like a toddler (E. Furman, 1981).

Many things may play a part in bringing about such developmental delays or arrests. Often they are related to the child experiencing too little urge satisfaction or too much urge stimulation. When children are expected to forego all satisfaction of an infantile urge before it even comes into its own in the course of their development, they may be unable to comply, or unable to channel and transform the pleasure appropriately, or they may comply but then need to go back to it when a later stress weakens their resources. For example,

Angela became toilet trained during her first year, before her pleasurable interest in bodily products emerged, but, in spite of mother's restrictions and prohibitions, she remained messy with food, untidy with her own and the family's belongings, and could not learn to use messy media in a creative way. The mother described her activity as being like a hurricane that leaves everything in a shambles in its wake. When Angela was four years old she was injured in an accident. She recovered her bodily health but reverted to wetting and soiling which continued until the mother sought professional help.

The opposite extreme, too much stimulation, may come about in several ways, but may interfere just as much with the child's ability to progress and to utilize his energy in new ways. Since infantile urges are usually so removed from what adults recognize as exciting, even parents may be unaware of how readily children are aroused and how easily they are overwhelmed by intense feelings which then preclude mastery. Thus, children may become overstimulated when left to enjoy their bodily pleasures for long periods (for example, to soil, wet, smear, or to play with their genitals) while their loved adults are absent or unavailable. More often people or experiences, unwittingly, overstimulate the child. This may apply to such things as parents' excessive and/or prolonged care of the child's body, especially of his rectal and genital areas (wiping, cleansing, applying ointments); frequent bodily fondling, kissing, and touching in affectionate interplays; wrestling and chasing games; bathing, toileting, dressing, and sleeping together which involve bodily contact and/or seeing each other naked; opportunity to witness adults' sexual intimacies or fights and arguments; repeated exposure to seeing or hearing incidents of a sexual nature or of hurting and being hurt through talk, TV movies, or books. It is of course impossible to protect children from everything that goes on in the world around them. It helps, however, to be aware of its impact on them. When youngsters have experienced things that may be hard for them to cope with, parents help by acknowledging their feelings (upset, confused, excited, scared), and by explaining matters calmly and simply to assist with mastery (R. A. Furman, 1994).

CAN ARRESTS IN THE DEVELOPMENT OF
THE URGES PERSIST INTO ADULTHOOD?
HOW DO THEY SHOW THEMSELVES AND
CAN THEY BE HELPED?

Such arrests do not necessarily correct themselves, and, unless understood and helped, may in one form or another continue to burden the child's and later adult's personality. For example, failure to shift the pleasure in curiosity and mastery from bodily to mental pursuits may interfere with the motivation to learn and work; prevalent persistence of infantile sexual pleasures in hurting and being hurt, or in looking and being looked at, may lead to a preference for perverse practices in lieu of adult genital sexual enjoyment. Continued pleasure in being contrary, in arguing and mental sparring may spoil the chance for cooperative caring relationships. Some adult couples fight and even hurt each other constantly, not because they don't like each other, but because they do so in an infantile way. Their inability to let go of each other often shows in remaining together, or in repeated reunions interspersed with separations, or in continued mutual harassment even after a divorce.

Many factors may contribute to interruptions in personality development in childhood, and many more shape their ultimate outcome in the adult. When grown-ups suffer from difficulties of this nature, they can get help through treatment with a psychiatrist, psychoanalyst, or psychologist.

NUDITY IS NATURAL. I THINK CHILDREN
SHOULD SEE THEIR PARENTS IN THE NUDE
FROM THE START BECAUSE THEN THEY
WILL NOT THINK OF IT AS SEXUAL.

Societies, and individuals within them, have adopted different attitudes to the infantile, pleasure-seeking urge of looking and being looked at, both in regard to its early focus on bodies and in regard to its diverted and transformed outlets, that is, the enjoyment of curiosity in general and of showing off in a nonbodily way, such as clothes, skills, and achievements. However, as with all urges, this one too is always subject to restrictions in one or another area. In this country the law prohibits nudity in public, except in specified places and by consenting adults, and custom encourages enjoyment of showing and admiration of nonbodily attributes, especially skills and achievements. By implication, the pleasurable excitement which accompanies the urge satisfaction is taken for granted but restricted to the privacy of home, club, or secluded beach. Other societies, and some individuals in our society, deal with this urge by allowing looking and being looked at in its original bodily form but prohibiting the exciting feelings that accompany it. This holds true in nudist colonies as well as in families which practice nudity. Looking and being looked at without excitement is not a natural, but an acquired attitude, and children have to learn it, with the help of their parents. It involves dealing with the excited feelings by such measures as suppression, diversion, or dulling. It is particularly hard for children to accomplish during the preschool years, when this urge is at its most intense, becomes somewhat less difficult during the later school years when it subsides, only to intensify again in adolescence when it reemerges along with the newly strong urge of genital sexuality. The child's difficulty in learning to cope in this way is often exacerbated by the fact that the parents do not recognize just how hard the task is and demand immediate, rather than gradual, success, while exposing him to a full measure of stimulation. Signs of the children's failure are commonly encountered: For example, continued enjoyment of looking and being looked at in secret, which may contribute to the later perversions of voyeurism and exhibitionism; "addiction" to watching TV; inability to ask about and understand sexual matters by means of words (not asking does not mean "knowing all about it" since the nature and functions of important internal organs cannot be deduced from visual observation); difficulty in diverting curiosity into self-motivated learning; inappropriate showing off, such as clowning or showing off in the bad sense of the term; and difficulty, even extreme shyness, in performing in front of others (as when called on to recite at school) or in taking pleasure in nonbodily showing off of skills and achievements.

It may seem ironic, but not surprising, that the same difficulties may result from educational methods which allow too much gratification as result from those which allow too little; prohibiting looking without giving verbal enlightenment may prove as unhelpful as giving the opportunity to see everything.

ISN'T CHILDREN'S CURIOSITY ABOUT BODIES, AS WELL AS THEIR TAKING THINGS APART, AN INTELLECTUAL INTEREST? THEY ARE NOT EXCITED, THEY ARE INQUISITIVE.

Children are both excited and inquisitive. When the excited aspect of their curiosity is not recognized, when it is overstimulated or harshly prohibited early on, the intellectual aspect may suffer. In normal development, the pleasure-seeking urges are a helpful companion for investing and furthering the intellectual functions. They make being inquisitive fun, just as they support need fulfillment and make eating fun. But they cannot play this part effectively, either when they are not allowed to participate at all during the initial development of a function or when they become so overstimulated that their energy cannot be transformed into nonbodily pleasure. In the former instance, learning and finding out may cease to provide satisfaction and will not be pursued; in the latter instance, the curiosity may remain excitedly focused on bodily matters and will not extend to learning and finding out about other things.

SHOULD YOUNG CHILDREN BE TOLD ABOUT SEXUAL INTERCOURSE?

Children are helped when their questions are answered simply, truthfully, and to the extent that they can understand and integrate information at a given time. When parents are in tune with their child, they sense this correctly from what the child says, from what they know he has observed and experienced, and from the way he acts and plays. They know that sexual matters are often hard to grasp (not only because they are intellectually difficult but also because they are linked with many intense feelings), that discussions therefore need to be followed up to clear up misunderstandings, and that it is important to find the right time and place for dealing with the topic privately. Most children have questions about how babies are made, can understand answers geared to their level, and can in that context also understand better that men's and women's bodies are different in order to fulfill this function.

Unfortunately, many parents were not verbally informed by their own parents and this makes it hard for them to be in tune with their child and to find the right words. They may feel tongue-tied and embarrassed, or they may become very "scientific" and give microscopic details about ova and sperms, or they may overwhelm their children with information they are not ready for. This is illustrated by the jocular story of the mother who, in response to the child's question of "Where did I come from?" launched into a lengthy account of procreation, at the end of which the child said, "Well, all I really wanted to know was whether I was born in Cleveland or in Chicago." It always helps to ascertain first just exactly what it is the child wants to know, how he came to wonder about it, what his own ideas are, how he arrived at his conclusions. If the child really wants to know "where I come from," it often suffices at first to tell him that it takes a Mommy and a Daddy, that they make a baby together when they love each other in a special way.

Children usually forget much of the specific sexual information the parents told them during the preschool years, but they do remember the most important things: that sexual matters are a private thing about which everyone has feelings, that it is all right to want to know and ask about them, and that the parents will answer inquiries in a helpful way and leave the child with a comfortable feeling about it.

HOW MUCH MASTURBATION IS "TOO MUCH"?

Some people are altogether opposed to children masturbating, others would place no restriction on it, and others yet are uncertain as to what approach to follow and how to gauge whether the child's masturbatory activities are within "normal" limits. Different customs and beliefs, as well as different attitudes and experiences in their individual lives, contribute to different ideas.

As we have noted earlier, children's self-comforting habits tend to follow the developmental phases of the pleasure-seeking urges, focusing first on the mouth, then successively on different bodily parts. For the preschooler and older child, his genitals are the main bodily pleasure zone and this manifests itself in masturbatory activities. Parents may occasionally notice their child masturbate in one form or another. However, after children are told, or deduce on their own, that this is a private matter, not appropriate in front of others, they usually limit themselves to times when they are alone. These are the times when self-comfort and discharge of minor tensions are helpful, for example before falling asleep. When masturbation serves the young child in this way, parents often do not even know about it.

However, when children are overstimulated, or worried about their bodies, or have missed their absent or unavailable parents too much, masturbation may intensify, as it becomes a way for the child to cope with these concerns. It may be an attempt to discharge excessive accumulated tensions, or to reassure himself of bodily intactness, or to compensate for the emotional loss of the parent. Since no amount of masturbation can effectively calm such concerns, it may then turn into an added worry for the child because he does not feel in control of it. Parents and educators usually notice this kind of masturbation because the child can no longer limit himself to privacy, and because it may interfere with the child's usual play and activities, through restlessness and diminished concentration. When the excited or worried feelings become so strong that they are master of the child, instead of the child being master of them, when they, so to speak, never leave him alone and overwhelm him, then masturbation is "too much." But this would not be an indication of too much fun and indulgence but of too much concern, and would warrant the parents' trying to understand and help, if need be with professional assistance.

ISN'T TV A BAD INFLUENCE ON CHILDREN, ESPECIALLY SINCE IT SHOWS SO MUCH VIOLENCE?

Television is not an unavoidable part of life. It does not impose itself on us willy-nilly. It is a controllable instrument that we use as and when we wish. A lot depends, therefore, on the parents' own TV watching habits and program preferences, and on their rules for the children's use of it.

With TV, as with all experiences, the parents are the child's natural shield against being overwhelmed and help in mastering stimuli. The parents judge which programs are suitable and, by sharing watching with the child or by knowing what is shown, assist him to understand it and to cope with the feelings it arouses. In this way, TV can serve as a means of entertainment and instruction (Hall, 1982a).

4
Putting Aggression to Use

In looking at aggression as an urge, an innate energy, we have already traced some of its developmental paths and seen how the growing personality uses it in helpful ways. We have touched on how it supports needs and need fulfillment: for example, by adding chewing and biting to satisfying independent eating, and by adding protest against hurt to self-protection. We have noted how, in the course of maturation, it links up with the phases of the pleasure-seeking urges. For example, during babyhood, when the mouth provides the most intense pleasurable satisfactions, the mouth is also used to discharge aggression through biting and screaming, and during the toddler period, when "being the boss" by messing and withholding, and by teasing and hurting, serves both to gain pleasure and to show anger—the very things that make the toddler so "positive" and "negative." In talking about frustrations we have seen, indirectly, how aggression assists in achieving satisfactions, how it helps us to clear obstacles and go after what we want, how in fact this is such an important role of aggression that some people view aggression only as a response to frustration. We have followed some of the ways in which aggression becomes channeled and transformed into activity, lends zest and initiative to what we do but, at the same time, loses its earlier destructive aspect: for example, in sports and bodily skills, in effective speech, and in grappling with problems through talking.

AGGRESSION IN THE SERVICE OF SELF-DEFENSE

In looking at aggression as a companion and ally to needs and pleasure-seeking urges, we have seen it linked to eating and to protesting bodily pain or discomfort, but have not yet stressed the prominent role aggression plays in every form of self-defense, one of our guardians of self-preservation. When our bodily or mental well-being is endangered, when our rights are disregarded, we normally get angry and stand up for ourselves: "I won't take that lying down. I'll do something about it." The baby is likely to scream, spit, and bite in self-defense. The toddler hits, kicks, pushes, and throws things. The older preschooler yells orders: "Stop it," "Get away," "No." Depending on the child and on the way he views the danger, he may do all those things.

In our society we very much go along with nature in this respect. We recognize a wide variety of individual rights, including the right to protect and defend oneself. But effective though it is, as well as legally permitted, self-defense does not consist of blind rage and does not allow indiscriminate means, nor is its goal necessarily to destroy the person or thing which endangers us. If we were to defend ourselves in such a manner, we could easily end up in greater danger than we were to start with. Good self-defense involves sizing up the situation realistically and using one's mobilized aggressive energy selectively, to achieve the best possible result. Sometimes this may indeed mean mustering full physical force to remove, incapacitate, even kill an attacker; sometimes it may mean a firm verbal command, or just a polite statement of protest. At other times, it may be best to run away or to get help; and there are also times when we have to keep our anger strictly in our thoughts and do nothing, lest we incur an even bigger injury. All this implies good control of aggression and being able to use it in a number of ways, through actions, words, or thoughts. It also implies other abilities, such as observing well and using good judgment. Endowment provides us with the necessary aggressive energy and, in the course of development, with several means of discharge; the inner control and know-how of using them appropriately is acquired primarily with the help of the parents, and other important adults, through the relationship with them (E. Furman, 1992, 1993).

It all starts with the parent's respect for the child, for the inviolate safety and integrity of his body, and dignity as a person. We have talked elsewhere (E. Furman, 1998a, 1998b) about how this attitude affects the parents' handling of the child's needs and of discipline, and we can now add to it the parents' necessary respect for the child's urges and feelings. This includes accepting the child's right to angry protest in self-defense when he feels that the parents are encroaching on his "space." The toddler who struggles to be his own person in body and the adolescent who struggles to be independent in mind and action feel particularly vulnerable. They protest constantly and keenly against everything they experience as taking over, imposing, interfering, restricting, and prohibiting on the part of the parents. But preschoolers and school-age children too are sensitive to not being considered and listened to, and not having their wishes, needs, and opinions taken into account. This does not mean that respectful parents don't say "no," that they allow their child to do what he wants, or that they let the child disregard *their* "space" in an inappropriate way. Realistic and necessary expectations have to be made and met in the interests of everyone's, including the child's, safety and well-being. Moreover, respect has to be mutual. The parents too have the right to protect themselves from the child's aggressive interference or abuse, while allowing him to speak up for himself or to use other age-appropriate means of self-defense.

When Alan was nine months old he was a healthy vigorous baby who screamed in loud protest when his mom kept him waiting, or when she tried to wash off his face while he was busy playing with something, or when his brother took away his toy. Mrs. B. certainly did not like Alan's screaming but she accepted it with equanimity, apologized for the various infringements, and tried to correct them. Brother had to return the toy to Alan and she herself, next time, did not surprise him with the washcloth on his face, but gave him a few words of preparation or waited for a more opportune moment. However, Mrs. B. did not let Alan bite. To the accompaniment of a firm "no," she would prevent or interrupt his biting by holding Alan at bay. In his second year, Alan sometimes hit out and kicked at his mom when he felt interfered with: for example, when she picked him up and carried him at a time when he wanted to walk, or when she took away the cookie box he had gotten off the shelf. Mrs. B. was glad that her little boy had progressed from screaming and biting to hitting out, but now that Alan had also begun to say a few words, she encouraged him to voice his protest verbally: "No hurting, Alan. You say 'no' to mommy. When you're angry you can tell me like I tell you." She offered him the simple expressions "no" and "angry" because these were her ways of addressing him when he made her angry. Other mothers prefer other words: *bad, mean, stop it*. All these are effective for registering and expressing angry protest and are easily learned even by toddlers with limited speech. "Mommy" and "no" are usually among their first words. It is a big step from physical to verbal expression of anger but, if it is in keeping with the parents' behavior to the child, he can usually master it during the preschool years. Saying how angry he is also helps the child to preserve his dignity when he still has to *do* what is required. Little Alan oftentimes stomped up the stairs with angry shouts of "No, I won't go." His mother did not mind his protest as long as he was making his way upstairs. Earlier, Alan, like most toddlers, used to respond to requests with a little delay or with doing just one more time whatever he had been asked not to do. Mrs. B. allowed him these face-saving gestures, but she was delighted when he followed her suggestion of protesting in words, and she praised him for it. Later Alan became more competent and less helpless, gained more confidence in himself as a person in his own right, and felt himself less easily threatened, but sometimes he still grumbled protests under his breath or indulged in a few angry thoughts when he had to comply with things that were not to his liking. Most times, though, he no longer viewed obeying as a humiliating "giving in." Even his verbal anger became less loud and he could state his complaints more clearly and politely. Disagreements between him and his parents were tolerated. They could be angry at each other without scenes or fights, and could still respect each other. The B.'s had helped their older boy in the same way and saw to it that, all along, the rules for standing up for oneself were the same between the brothers as between child and parent.

When children are allowed and helped to defend themselves against their parents and siblings and are treated respectfully by them, they learn quickly how to stand up for their rights with outsiders and how to use means of self-defense which are appropriate to the situation. Without help within the family, children have a hard time learning to defend themselves in the community. They may not be able to stand up for themselves and become easy victims, or they may vent their stored up anger against others indiscriminately, either in retaliation for minor encroachments or as bullies of weaker and smaller peers. For example, they may angrily clobber another child for trying to take their toy instead of holding on to it with a firm, "No, it's mine," or they may lash out with full force on the pretext of, "He hit me first," or even of, "He was going to hit me," instead of a firm, "Stop it," or, if necessary, pushing the other child away or even getting help.

By the time children are in public school they have usually learned to just *think* how angry they are at, say, a teacher. On the one hand this is a mark of achievement in inner control, on the other hand, knowing that he is angry, and what he is angry about, is also the mark of being a person in his own right, and is a big help in figuring out what best to do about a situation.

USING AGGRESSION TO ATTAIN PLEASURES

Aggression not only serves us to defend ourselves against others but to attain pleasures for ourselves. The satisfactions we want are rarely readily at hand. Usually there are obstacles to overcome and, for the child especially, one of the obstacles often is the parents. Most parents appreciate their child as a "go-getter." They are glad when he enjoys lots of things and activities, goes out in a determined way to achieve them, and does not easily give up in the face of hardship from within or without. Parents are not always so glad to see their young child go after his pleasure with similar determination, in part because they disapprove of some of his infantile pleasures, and in part because the child's determination is so aggressive that he sometimes forges ahead without regard for property, people, or even his own safety. The toddler who is determined to get the cookie box, pulls up a chair, climbs the shelves, throws the box down, and scatters the contents endangers himself, may ruin the box, and may deprive the rest of the family of their share of cookies. And if the same toddler still loves to tease and torment, he may go after his pleasure with similar gusto till he has worn out his mother or gotten himself scratched by the cat. When the parents interfere and stop him before he is in big trouble, he is likely to get very angry at them and show it, in typical toddler fashion, with more angry responses. The preschooler too goes after his wants in aggressive ways. In pursuit of being first and best, he often pushes others aside ruthlessly to "get first in line," cheats to win a game, brags shamelessly, and "one-ups" himself by belittling the others, often with humiliating singsong, "Nya, nya, you are the last."; "I know how to skip. Look at me! You don't even know how to. You are a baby!"

If the parents squash the child's aggression in attaining pleasures too much and too harshly, he will not have it available in the form of proper determination. He may give up at the first hurdle, whining "I can't do it" or crying "*You* do it, it's too hard for me." By contrast, if they allow the child free reign to pursue his infantile pleasures all along, by whatever means he chooses, he may continue to do so in his ruthless infantile way. Many parents, however, do find the difficult middle road: They frustrate calmly and gradually, allow verbal anger, and point the way to more acceptable ways. They also provide a model in their own behavior toward the child and others. When the child cheats during a game, they don't get angry, punish, or threaten never to play with him again, but say something like, "Hey, I also don't like losing, but I still stick by the rules. It's hard but you'll learn and then the other kids will really want to play with you. They'll say 'He plays fair, he's fun to play with.' So let's put back that card, start over again, and this time you'll do it the fair way, like a big guy." And when the child manages to survive a lost game, fairly played, with a mere verbal, "Oh, shucks, I hate losing. I never win," his father even praises him and lets him show off his big-boy achievement.

AGGRESSION FUELING ACTIVITIES

As some personality tools such as motility develop, it is easy to see how much aggression initially contributes to their exercise. A toddler on the go is a pleasure to behold, in that he is so determinedly active, but he is also a menace, in that he avoids nothing and stops at nothing. Less obviously, this happens with other tools too. Speech is used in anger, and we even encourage that, but young children's verbal anger is far from polite. They may be angrily loud, say mean things, threaten, hurl insults, and voice all kinds of evil wishes. Their ability to observe and think is likewise often aggressive. They insist on finding out and knowing things, won't take no for an answer, and often seem to observe and reason especially keenly in the areas where we would prefer them not to. Their ears and eyes are tuned not to miss out on the weaknesses and troubles of the adults, on shortcomings in their appearance and behavior, and they often startle and embarrass us with their frankness: "How come, grandma, that your hands have spots all over them, and your neck is all hanging down? Is it because you're so old? Are you going to die soon?"; "My daddy didn't want to go to the block party because they are all a bunch of busybodies. It's true, I heard him tell my mom."

It is tempting to "jail" the toddler in a playpen, to punish a youngster for impolite and angry talk, to forbid him to listen and want to know, or to persuade him that his observations are incorrect or his feelings nonexistent: "You don't really hate the baby, you *like* him." Fortunately, most parents, though distressed by the aggressive onslaught of the child's new abilities, also enjoy his spunkiness a bit and sense that it will stand him in good stead and lose its initial abrasiveness, if they guide it rather than altogether suppress it. They help the toddler go from freewheeling motility to learning motor skills (going up and down the stairs, tricycling, rolling a ball); they point out to the preschooler that bigger people are more polite when they are angry; they provide opportunities for the child to observe and learn other things and explain about some matters being private within the family and about hurting people's feelings. Even the best parents are not always so patient and thoughtful. A sense of humor helps to keep things in perspective.

At times, young children's aggression can be unprovoked and diffuse, discharged "all over" and against everyone and everything. This is especially evident with toddlers, but also with older children at vulnerable times—when they are tired at the end of the day, when they are getting over an illness, when they have been "cooped up," when their opportunities for activity have been curtailed, or when their means of control have been diminished by stress. It usually does not help them to "blow off steam" and "get it out of their system." Aggressive behavior does not exhaust itself, but tends to stimulate more aggressive behavior. Channeling aggression into activities at such times is more helpful. At first the activity may serve as an outlet for aggression, but in time the activity can absorb the aggression and transform its energy into helpful fuel, especially when a loved person supports and encourages the child (E. Furman, 1992, 1993).

Three-year-old Henry often spent part of his nursery school day hitting each child as he passed by. The teacher forbade this and offered him a hammering toy. She showed him how he could bang in its colored pegs. Henry liked his teacher, watched her using the toy with interest, but at first refused to participate. One day, however, Henry picked up on her encouragement, really settled down to it, and left the other children alone. As he hammered away, he called out the children's names with each bang "Joseph," "Keith," "Barbara." He had taken a small but significant step from aggression to activity. In time Henry came to like hammering for its own sake. With the teacher's help, he branched out into carpentry. His goal was no longer to attack children but to produce little wooden airplanes and other projects which he cherished and which earned him much admiration.

AGGRESSION AS A PART OF THE
PARENT–CHILD RELATIONSHIP

It is sometimes thought that parents and children don't or shouldn't get angry at each other because they are so close, so intimately tied by bonds of mutual need, dependency, care, and love. Actually, the reverse is true: We don't get anywhere near as angry at people who don't matter to us as we do at those who mean a lot to us. The closer our ties and the more intimate our togetherness, the more we invest our relationships, not only with love but also with anger. There are many reasons for this, among which are the following: When we love someone very much, we want him or her to love us back just as much, and when it seems to us that the person does not fully reciprocate, we get very frustrated and hence angry ("If you loved me, you would do as I want you to"). Also, a close relationship always implies that we need the other person, depend on him or her. This carries with it a feeling of being at the partner's mercy, being helpless without him or her. Nothing makes us more angry than being helpless. Moreover, being lovingly close always demands a measure of surrendering, of sharing, and of giving up of oneself. This easily conflicts with our other need of being a separate independent individual. We get angry when we feel that the demands of loving and being loved interfere too much with our "space " Then we want to get away and "do our own thing." At other times we may measure ourselves competitively against the loved one, feel envious and angrily wish to take away his or her advantages, instead of giving more of ourselves.

No relationship, not even that of husband and wife, is closer in all these respects than the relationship between parent and child. They, who began their relationship as a part of one another's body, sense most keenly their helpless need for and dependence on each other, experience most readily rejection and frustration when the mutual demands of compliance and surrender go unmet, and, at the same time and because of their very closeness, feel so easily that the loved partner encroaches upon and usurps their "space" of individuality. It is not only the children who need and depend on the parents, demand their full loving absorption, and yet struggle for independence and resent parental interference. The same applies to the parents. They too need and depend on their child, feel hurt and frustrated when he asserts his self-sufficiency and independence, and at other times get angry at his "demandingness" when it threatens their individual integrity: "He doesn't leave me alone. He always wants something. I can't even be myself for a minute." And just as children get envious of their parents, so parents get envious of their children, envious of their youth, of their being taken care of, of their good fortune and comforts, often of the very advantages they, the parents, lovingly brought about. Perhaps the strange part is not that parents and children get angry at each other, but that their relationship engenders so much mutual pleasure and satisfaction that, for the most part, it manages to resolve and overcome these conflicts and subdue the anger it generates.

And this indeed is one of the most crucial tasks of the parent–child relationship: to "tame" aggression through love. Parents usually do get angry at the child, but the constancy and strength of their love for him helps them to be angry in such a way that they do not harm him and do not altogether stop loving him. In the process, they help their child to achieve the same mastery over his anger at them. It is not an easy task. Young children's anger easily overrides their love, knows little or no consideration, and at the least frustration, would prompt them to discard the loved one. However much they love their parents, when young children are angry they do not hesitate to lash out at them, and are often quite ready to exchange the "bad" mother or father of the moment for another one who may prove to be more gratifying. The bread and butter always seems better at the Jones's. In addition, toddlers tinge their love with aggression, so that even when they do love they make hurting and being hurt, bodily and mentally, part and parcel of it. Their hug is often hard to tell from an assault. Modifying the expression of anger so as not to hurt, forgiving, loving others in spite of their faults, and being capable of the kind of constant love which even tames anger, these are slow and difficult achievements. Not all of us reach these goals but, insofar as we do reach them it is with the help of our relationship with our parents (E. Furman, 1992, 1993).

When this relationship is consistent and good enough, and when the parents have, to a sufficient extent, mastered their own aggression vis-à-vis the child, the pleasures and satisfactions of mutual caring exercise a powerful pull. For its sake children want to modify their anger, want to master it like the admired parents, and, ultimately, adopt their standards for themselves and make them a part of their conscience. The parents help by setting an example, by praising and disapproving, and by adapting their expectations to the child's capabilities. That is why they don't become too alarmed at their youngsters' furies, let their children be angry at them in words, though not in deeds, and act so as to assure them that their love will survive it all: "Well, you are real mad at me now but we also still like each other and that's why we don't hurt each other and stay together." Even when the parents are mature and can rely on good inner controls, it is not easy for them to master their anger at the child and to help him master his. The primitive intensity of the child's anger often threatens their adult controls and seduces them to respond to the child at his level: "I don't know what happened to me. I just lost my cool." This is one reason why adults are often less masters of their anger with their children than they are with adults, or even with other people's children. Fortunately, they do not have to be perfect, only good enough.

When children can learn to tame their anger toward the parents, the first and most important loved ones, it will stand them in good stead in their other and later relationships. Properly tamed aggression will also help them to develop a conscience that can effectively guide their behavior. The parents' values and prohibitions in regard to anger form a part of the child's conscience, but it is also shaped by the way the child feels about the parents and by how he views them. If the child is intensely angry himself, he is apt to think of them as "mean," to perceive them as very critical and punitive. Children sometimes feel that their parents are much stricter than the parents think they are, and this is often due to the fact that the children still judge the parents' anger at them by their own anger at the parents. When children struggle persistently with intense anger at the parents without being able to modify it, their conscience may come to resemble parents who are seen as terribly strict and unforgiving. Such an exaggeratedly harsh conscience, whose anger is untamed, is not a helpful guide. It may set unreasonably high standards and enforce them relentlessly. When its plagued owner inevitably fails to live up to them, it never forgives transgressions, is not satisfied with atonement and reparation, and never lets one feel good.

WHEN AGGRESSION GETS IN THE WAY

Aggressive urges do not always find their way into useful channels, do not always contribute appropriately to self-preservation, well-being, and acceptable social conduct, nor do they, in all people, fuel functions and activities in modified and transformed ways. In fact, the unhelpful, destructive manifestations of aggression are often the only ones noticed, and have earned aggression a thoroughly bad name.

We see unhelpful aggression when it is untamed by love and erupts in tempers and violent attacks on people and things, untempered by consideration and pity, or when, accompanied by pleasurable excitement, it seeks gratification in hurting and being hurt, in torturing, tormenting, and perverse sexual practices. When these behaviors, which are normally seen only in toddlers, are observed in older children and adults, they tell us that a part of the personality has remained a toddler while other parts have grown up. The more advanced parts may function separately and well at times, but they may also interact with the toddler part and render it much more troublesome. They lend it greater physical and mental strength and powerful means of expression which were not available to the toddler. A twenty-five-year-old "toddler" is much more dangerous than a two-year-old.

We see unhelpful aggression discharged through personality tools and activities instead of becoming modified and serving them as fuel and initiative; for example, some children misuse motility in sports as a license to barge into, attack, and ruthlessly subdue others, instead of using it as a means to exercise a skill (every sports coach knows and dreads such individuals). Likewise, observing and thinking can be used merely for destructive purposes instead of constructive and adaptive ones ("He is very smart and he thinks well, but all he uses it for is mischief and troublemaking"). Even speech, which is to serve as a tool for mastering aggression and expressing it appropriately, is often misused through "foul-mouthing," or by turning words into weapons to hurt, humiliate, and torment, to bite in sarcasm, or to strip others and lay bare their inadequacies in order to belittle them.

We see unhelpful aggression turned against the self, either physically, as in accident proneness and some forms of suicide, or mentally, as in unjustified and exaggerated self-criticism, torturing guilt, low self-esteem, and inability to enjoy successes. And we see its destructive impact on the personality when it interferes with need-fulfillment (for example, when excessive mouth anger inhibits chewing and prevents enjoyable eating), and when it encroaches upon pleasurable comfort habits (for example, when children pull out their hair, bang their heads hard, bite their nails to the quick, or scratch themselves until they bleed) (E. Furman, 1984b).

We are less often aware of the damaging effects of excessively inhibited aggression, of the ways in which it deprives children of zest and initiative, contributes to helplessness and hopelessness in the face of life's daily tasks and challenges, and interferes with feeling good and having fun.

Of course, aggression is not solely responsible for these and similar difficulties. The makeup of our personalities is so complex that we can never attribute a piece of behavior such as aggression to a single isolated factor, but it can and does play an important part.

How does aggression get to show itself in such unhelpful ways? Here again, many factors within and without the child interact to shape the individual outcome in a personality, but we can pinpoint a few things which make it difficult for aggression to be appropriately channeled and modified. We have already implicitly referred to a number of them. When we remind ourselves of parents' helpful measures, their opposites are obviously unhelpful. Among these would be the lack of a consistent parent–child relationship, that is, one interrupted too often by temporary separations or emotional withdrawals, by multiple caretakers, or by permanent changes in parenting persons. Even a consistent parent–child relationship may not be good enough, in the sense of not providing a sufficient loving investment and pleasurable experiences in meeting the child's bodily and emotional needs. Excessive aggression may be the outcome of diminished opportunities for love and pleasure. Some severely destructive delinquent children actually do suffer from a lack of love and cannot be helped to modify their aggressive behavior until and unless they have an opportunity to form a consistent good enough relationship with parental figures (A. Freud, 1949a). Such a relative lack of good enough experiences may, however, not be due to deficits in parental handling or to lack of a relationship. It may be caused by painful illnesses and their treatments, or by congenital abnormalities which make it impossible for the child to feel good. The parents' care may not suffice to counteract the hurting and frustrating experiences a child has to endure, through repeated surgeries from early on, or as a result of major handicaps. Even limited illnesses can interfere with important needs and functions, such as when a baby's eating always hurts and hence cannot bring pleasure or absorb aggression, or when a toddler cannot walk and therefore cannot channel aggression into motor control. However, some difficulties may also arise within the context of a consistent and good enough parental relationship with a healthy child, and may reflect unhelpful aspects of parent–child interactions. For example, the parents' handling of their own aggression may set an unhelpful example to emulate (they may be explosively angry); or the parents may not allow the child enough age-appropriate expression of anger and thus block the channels of discharge that could lead to mastery ("You must never be angry at your parents"); or they may not provide opportunities for the child to invest aggression in activity (perhaps by confining a toddler too long in his bed, playpen, or carriage); or they may insist on "taking over" and deprive the child of active independence. Most parents err in one or another direction at times. Usually though, they also "read" the child's response and readjust their handling accordingly. As long as the basic relationship is a healthy one and parents correct their mistakes, children forgive their parents and progress in their development after a little setback.

IS IT HELPFUL FOR PARENTS TO LET THE CHILD "TAKE OUT" HIS ANGER ON SOMETHING ELSE, INSTEAD OF DIRECTING IT AGAINST THEM?

It is helpful for parents to provide opportunities for physical and other activities which can absorb aggressive energy, but this proves helpful only in addition to, not instead of, allowing and encouraging children to express anger in words directly to the parents. There are good reasons for this:

1. We can only come to terms with our anger when we are fully aware of whom it is aimed at and why. Misdirected anger, anger aimed at the wrong object for the wrong reason, remains active and can never stop or be modified. When parents encourage their child to hit the punching bag instead of them, they advise the child to misdirect his anger and do not help him to control and modify its form of expression. Unfortunately, parents and children often unwittingly collude in such misdirection of anger. Parents tend to prefer, consciously or unconsciously, that their children not be angry at them and blame them, and children are only too ready to redirect their anger from the loved, needed, and perhaps feared parents to less important "victims." For example, parents often like to think that the child is angry at their new baby rather than being angry at them for bringing it into the family, although even the tiniest child knows that a baby has not arrived of its own will and that the parents would not keep and love it unless they had wanted it. The child, for his part, may prefer to be angry at the baby instead of at the parents, lest he endanger his relationship with them which already appears threatened by the arrival of the newcomer. The misdirected anger at the baby may, however, remain active and will continue to burden the relationship between the siblings. Many ongoing sibling rivalries originate from anger that really belongs to the parents. Some parents do not even accept their child's anger at the baby, but "let" him be aggressive to pets or to others outside the family. Such misdirected anger may protect the family relationships but leads to trouble in other relationships as well as

to possible difficulties with the community and its laws. In these instances unexpressed anger at the authority of the parents turns into anger at society.

2. Anger against the parents has the best chance of being tamed by love, an important step in mastery. When parents divert the child's anger, even to a punching bag, the aggressive expression remains physical and does not become tamed, channeled into words, and tempered by consideration for the loved one. Children are then in danger of dividing up love and anger and, in order to keep some of their relationships "pure," have to keep "bad guys" forever at hand as targets for the other side of their mixed feelings. Such a solution is not helpful, can lead to intolerance and prejudice, and accounts to some extent for the fact that some kind and nice persons behave in a very ruthless, vindictive way to certain individuals or groups of people.

3. Aggression is most successfully channeled into activities when a portion of it is allowed direct expression. Activities can absorb and modify only a certain amount of aggressive energy. When all of a child's anger is to be invested and discharged through activities, the process may fail; either activities may not become invested enough and are not practiced because they do not feel satisfying, or they remain a form of aggressive discharge instead of using modified energy and serving as skills.

ARE TEMPER TANTRUMS ALWAYS A TODDLER FORM OF AGGRESSION?

The typical toddler temper is a short outburst of aggressive behavior which the child readily overcomes and in time masters as he learns to express anger in words. Temper tantrums, by contrast, represent, at any age, an overwhelming of the personality that leave the child exhausted, frightened, weepy, unhappy, and in need of comfort. Such temper tantrums may be due to a "volcanic" outburst of small amounts of anger which have gone unexpressed and have accumulated until their force sweeps aside all barriers, either unprovoked at the time, or in response to a minor frustration. These pathological accumulations and discharges can be prevented when children are helped to recognize all the events and situations that cause them to be angry and are encouraged to express their anger piecemeal at the time when it arises.

In young children especially, but sometimes also at a later age, temper tantrums of this nature can also represent anxiety attacks, rather than outbursts of aggression. Whereas the signs of adult anxiety attacks are usually vague fear, palpitations, and increased perspiration, children's anxiety attacks characteristically take the form of exhausting temper tantrums. Only close and knowledgeable observation can succeed in distinguishing an anxiety attack from a volcanic outburst of aggression. Both, however, require help and should not be treated as mere naughtiness.

DON'T CHILDREN OFTEN DO NAUGHTY THINGS, NOT OUT OF ANGER, BUT TO GET ATTENTION?

In some families children find that being "good" makes the parents turn away from them, whereas being "bad" attracts their concern. It is a pity when children feel they have to pay the price of parents' anger and punishment to gain an intense close interaction with them. Sometimes this happens with parents who are depressed or who, without realizing it, tend to withdraw emotionally; for example, a mother, while on the phone, may become completely absorbed in her conversation and literally forget her child. By contrast, most mothers, even while on the phone, keep an alert mental link with their child, aware all the time of what he is doing, nodding to him, listening to signs of his activity, knowing when the child really needs them, and at the right time, interrupting their phone call to help him. When children "act up" to get attention they often indicate that they feel the parent is not reliably available to help them with inner and outer dangers. Their naughtiness, though enjoyed in one way, is also an SOS signal, a sign that the parents leave him too much to his own devices and fail to meet his need for consistent caring investment (R. A. Furman and E. Furman, 1984).

DOES ONE FEEL ANGRY WHEN ONE TAKES
THE INITIATIVE OR IS VERY COMPETITIVE IN
SPORTS, IN SCHOOL, OR IN WORK?

When aggression is appropriately modified and absorbed in activities it is no longer "angry" and is not felt as such. It may be very active and forceful but stays within the limits of social rules and laws and is not devoid of consideration for others. However, aggression is not always so well absorbed and may contain a great deal more of the original destructive anger than a person is aware of. We can, and do, act aggressively without feeling angry at times. Children quite sincerely sometimes deny being angry even when engaged in very destructive behavior, and so do adults. Parents may be very humiliating, restrictive, punitive, and without knowing how aggressive they are, may actually think they are acting "for the good of the child" (see also chapter 5).

CHILDREN ARE SOMETIMES AGGRESSIVE
AND EVEN DELINQUENT THOUGH THEIR
PARENTS ARE KIND, LAW-ABIDING CITIZENS.
HOW DOES THIS HAPPEN?

Each of these situations needs to be explored and understood individually and would, no doubt, reveal different factors at work. In my therapeutic work with such families, I have learned about some of them. For example, sometimes children's unmodified anger at the parents manifested itself in opposition to everything the parents stood for and the children's troublesome behavior, like the toddler's, served as their weapon to hurt the parents; some parents acted very differently with their children than they did with people socially or in their work and, as a result, the children's aggressive behavior actually did reflect the parents' handling of them, although an outsider would not have seen that. In some cases, the parents had experienced, and resented, a lot of hardship in their growing up, and, wanting to spare their children, made no expectations, set no limits, and condoned inappropriate behavior in their youngsters. They usually did not realize either that they vicariously enjoyed the children's aggression or that they were indirectly very aggressive to them by not helping them to develop well. Some parents were very upright citizens but did not maintain a consistent and good enough relationship with the child. A wonderful parent who is never there cannot help his child to emulate him. In some instances, children's aggressive or delinquent difficulties were related to identifications with similar characteristics of earlier parent figures they had since lost (a nanny or other caregiver, or a previous parent lost through death, divorce, or adoption). Most often several of these and additional circumstances interacted to account for the unfortunate but nevertheless understandable results.

ISN'T AGGRESSIVE–DELINQUENT BEHAVIOR CAUSED BY POVERTY AND SOCIAL INEQUALITIES?

These factors add special and powerful frustrations that arouse a great deal of anger. A person who could cope with his anger under ordinary circumstances may not be able to do so under conditions of such additional stress. However, even the most extreme socioeconomic hardships and personal misfortunes do not drive every sufferer to aggressive–delinquent behavior. We therefore should regard socioeconomic hardships as endangering stress factors but not as causes in themselves. This is likewise true of other stress factors, such as "bad company."

IS DELINQUENCY ALWAYS DUE TO LACK OF INNER CONTROL OF AGGRESSION?

Delinquency may actually be caused by a person's unrecognized guilt which demands punishment for him. We noted earlier that young school-age children quite commonly commit minor delinquencies, such as theft of small articles, playing with matches, or damaging objects they are not supposed to handle. They usually leave clues and, unlike "real" delinquents, are easily detected by their caring adults. These children often struggle with the demands of a newly taken in, harsh, and ever critical conscience. Without being aware of their inner turmoil or motivations, they may temporarily stave off and satisfy the inner voice of self-criticism by inviting and receiving punishment from the outside. Usually these behaviors subside when the child's conscience becomes better integrated into his personality and serves more effectively as a guide to conduct. In some individuals such a guilt problem may persist, along with repeated attempts to appease it with the help of getting punished (S. Freud, 1916; E. Furman, 1980, 1998b).

The police receive many unsolicited "confessions" and self-indictments for crimes that people only heard about but never committed—another instance of guilt driven behavior. Many of us can sympathize with such people because we sometimes feel like criminals even though we did not commit a real crime. For example, many people feel guilty when approached and questioned by police or other authorities even when they have ostensibly done nothing wrong. And there are few children who do not anticipate being accused of something when they are called to the principal's office, even though it may turn out that he gives them a commendation.

CAN TROUBLES WITH AGGRESSION BE OUTGROWN OR CORRECTED LATER ON? DO WE REALLY LEARN ALL ABOUT HANDLING AGGRESSION WHEN WE ARE LITTLE?

We do not learn all about aggression from and with our parents. They lay the important foundation. They help us take the crucial first steps. Building inner controls, finding appropriate pathways of expression, investing anger in ever new activities, adjusting our values and standards to the changing demands of living, and coping with the many situations of stressful frustration and hardship which fate inevitably imposes on everyone at times, including the special stress of learning how to deal with our anger at our children, these all are lifelong personality undertakings. They are influenced by many relationships and events and require ongoing effort and changes on our part.

Some difficulties with aggression in the course of development are temporary and are overcome. Others may become lasting or exacerbated. Individuals and their circumstances vary greatly, and it is therefore unwise to generalize. However, most often difficulties with aggression can be helped with psychological treatment if they have arisen in the context of a consistent and good enough early relationship. The most incorrigible problems with aggression are ultimately rooted in a lack of such a relationship during childhood.

5

Feelings

Feelings are what makes life rich. When we can experience them deeply, in all their variety and intensity, in all their many shades of happiness and misery, we truly live fully. This does not depend on how many adventures we encounter or how many blows fate metes out to us. Some people lead ostensibly very "exciting" lives, or very trying ones, but they remain emotionally poor and empty because their feelings are shallow or flat, or but briefly stirred. By contrast, other people's lives may seem very sheltered and uneventful, but may yet be filled to the brim with a wealth of deep and rich emotional experiences—the stuff that wisdom is made of. Nor do the riches of feelings depend on intelligence, intellect, and knowledge. True feelings do not require academic know-how or scientific proofs. As long as we have the ability to be aware of them and to bear them, they tell us correctly what goes on in our own bodies and minds, what other people's motivations and behaviors are about, how we relate with them and with the world around us. They enable us to experience and appreciate all the satisfactions and dissatisfactions, to know what we like and don't like, and they guide our thoughts and actions accordingly. Feelings constitute our emotional lives, some would say our souls. They keep us in touch with the workings of our vital energies, let us know about our needs and urges, enable us to enjoy meeting their demands, or feel angry and unhappy when we can't meet them

We "know" of our need for sleep when we *feel* tired, which prompts us to lie down. We enjoy sleeping well and are disgruntled when we can't sleep well, and we know when we are slept out because we no longer feel tired. And it's the same way with feeling hungry or feeling pain. When people gauge their need for sleep, food, or any other need "by the book," that is, by their learned knowledge about what their body needs, then everything they do about their needs and need fulfillment becomes a required chore, a duty imposed from without, and ceases to be an enriching emotional experience. How different it is when we go to bed because we feel tired and pleasurably anticipate a good sleep, from when we tell ourselves (or are told) that we now have to lie down and sleep because that's what our body needs. How different it is when we feel hungry, prepare what tastes good, and then eat it with relish, from when we eat, "at the right time," the prescribed essential vitamins, proteins, and carbohydrates, regardless of appetite. When needs are gauged and satisfied by knowledge alone, they preserve life but hardly make it worth living. Of course, feelings don't always add pleasure. When needs can't be met or met well, when we can't go to sleep when we are tired or can't sleep well, can't eat when we are hungry or can't eat what we want, we feel angry, miserable, irritable, desperate. But at least we are *we*, persons with a mind and will of our own, even with an unhappiness of our own. Without these feelings life is lackluster, wishy-washy, and we are less of a somebody. Even with a very young child, when he is really enjoying his meal or is really angry or sad when he can't have what he wants, we can't help but respect him, and people often comment "He sure is all there, isn't he."

This goes for the urges too, both in their original and in their modified forms. Feelings inform us of their promptings and enable us to experience their satisfactions and frustrations. When sexual activities are performed with little or no accompanying feelings, they become mere mechanical exercises. As such they are either rendered uninteresting and are given up, or are endlessly sought out and repeated in the vain hope for a more meaningful, satisfying experience next time. In either case, sexuality without feelings adds little to living, no rich pleasure and warm subtleties of loving, no pain of frustration or pangs of longing or jealousy. Likewise, when we cannot feel angry, we may not be able to act angry to defend our legitimate interests, or we may be very aggressive without knowing it, but neither lets us feel alive. We may not like feeling angry, yet may even then realize that getting "good and mad" has something invigorating and satisfying to it, and is often preferable to the mere indifference of "I don't mind," "I don't care."

This also applies to the many subtler feelings, derived from excitement or aggression, which have infused our personality functions and activities and which make their exercise worthwhile for us. Talking, thinking, doing, working, and pursuing hobbies all make us feel, and that is an important reason why we seek them out and why we miss them when there is no chance to engage in them. Sometimes we love them or agonize over them, sometimes they quietly please or irritate us. Good feelings or bad, satisfying or frustrating, how empty and dull life would be without them.

As for relationships, feelings are the essence of them. They enrich us with their fondnesses, enjoyments, hatreds, sadnesses, loves, irritating tensions, envies and jealousies, delights and tendernesses, and a whole host of other feelings besides. Even when a relationship is broken, it leaves us with pleasurable and painful feeling memories to fill the void, and that's why having had something and lost it is so much better than never to have had anything at all.

Moreover, true feelings, fully felt, give us a sense of certainty, a trust in ourselves and what we are about, and a "feel" about people and events. They help us to be masters of ourselves. Even when we feel helpless and know it, we are more in charge of ourselves than when we feel nothing.

And yet, our innate potential for having feelings and using them to enrich and serve us is not realized at birth and does not mature of itself. Like most of personality functioning, it has to be nurtured in the soil of continuous and good enough relationships and gradually mastered in order to come to fruition. At best, its developmental process is surprisingly fragile, buffeted from within and without, and easily suffers stunting and distortion.

FEELINGS AND BODILY RESPONSES

Feelings arise from the body and, to an extent, always remain linked to it. Very young babies have bodily sensations and discharge them in a variety of bodily ways. The first primitive mental experiences of feeling good and feeling bad accompany bodily processes, and are, perhaps, the first indications of the emergence of a mental self. The baby's smile is initially a bodily response to digestive relaxation and comfort. Parents rightly herald it as a milestone when it begins to appear as an expression of mental feeling in interaction with the smiling mother and, later, in spontaneous recognition of her.

Everyone who has taken full care of a baby knows that he looks most like a person, not when he is very excited or very distressed, but when he simply feels good. This "feeling good" comes when he feels "on top of things," when his discomforts are at a minimum and his pleasures are not very intense. This state of mind usually does not last very long. Even an older baby, who can already sustain and show a much greater amount of enjoyment, becomes bodily distressed and soon overwhelmed when the pleasure reaches a certain intensity; for example, a baby may gurgle, laugh, and sparkle when bounced on his father's knees, but if Dad continues the fun too long or goes about it too vigorously, the baby suddenly wrinkles up his face in distress, starts to writhe and cry, cannot be easily comforted into relaxation, and may even end up in an inconsolable paroxysm of screaming and thrashing. Mother then tends to scold Dad, "You got him much too excited," to which Dad defends himself with "But he loved it," and she retorts, "Not that much of it." She is annoyed because she knows that her overwhelmed baby will sleep fitfully, be unable to feed comfortably, and is likely to have gas pains. A baby's ability to feel bad mentally (that is, without marked bodily distress) develops even more slowly. A hungry baby may look unhappy and cry moderately for a very short while, but beyond that, if left to himself he becomes a screaming writhing bundle, and if mother tries to feed him in that state, he either won't take it in or will throw up and have a tummy ache. In short, feeling good and tolerating feeling good, encompassing it as a mental emotional experience, works at first only for small amounts of pleasurable sensations, and takes even longer to achieve in regard to unpleasurable ones. In time, however, the ability to feel increases and, in turn, becomes a means of coping with ever larger amounts of sensations and ever more intense ones. The feeling, as it were, gathers up and holds the sensations and gives them a mental pathway of discharge, with limited bodily involvement.

Overstimulated and distressed babies come to feel good, and bad, much later and, in extreme cases, not at all. They remain at the mercy of their sensations, showing labile extremes of excitement and distress but discharging them primarily through bodily processes. They tend to be tense, are hard to comfort, and respond to the least increase in inner and outer stimuli with troubles in sleeping, feeding, digesting, eliminating, with skin discomforts, and/or excessive random motility. Even under ordinary conditions, older babies, toddlers, and preschoolers still tend to show strong feelings with their bodies. This commonly manifests itself as lack of appetite, tummy pains, constipation or diarrhea, vomiting, feeling ill, being tired or restlessly hyperactive, and suffering from itching and skin discomforts. In response to a reprimand, three-year-old Wayne said to his mother angrily, "You, you, you make my tummy ache." He was not bodily ill but still felt his anger in a bodily way. The sooner children are helped to know their feelings and to express them effectively in words, the sooner are their bodily processes freed from the burden of discharging them (E. Furman, 1992, 1993).

Many adults have not achieved sufficiently effective mental pathways and experience bodily symptoms instead of or along with feelings. Common difficulties of this kind are "nervous" indigestion and "tension" headaches. In situations of extreme stress everyone is apt to notice their intensified bodily responses, and stress as such is known to trigger or aggravate many illnesses. The intimate link between feelings and the innermost workings of our bodies is also preserved through language. Feelings are "a matter of the heart"; we have "heartfelt sympathy" and "gut reactions"; we say, "He makes me sick," "It's yucky," "That's disgusting, it turns my stomach," "It gives me the chills," "It's a pain." For the most part though, when we use such phrases we describe our feelings and no longer experience them bodily.

NURTURING FEELINGS

By feeling with her baby, the mothering person plays an important part in helping him to feel. She feels her infant's capacity to tolerate pleasurable and distressing sensations and tries to make sure that they don't exceed that level. At the same time she contains his feelings for him and helps him to tolerate them. When the baby feels good, she feels good, and when he feels bad, she does too. But she feels it all mainly in her mind (or should we say "heart"?), and although she expresses her feeling through her facial features and perhaps through words, she is calm enough to convey an attitude of "This is okay. This doesn't throw me. I can manage this." For the infant who scans mother's face, is tuned to the emotional variations of her voice, and senses her body tone, this is both an assurance and a model. But mother often goes a step further and literally helps her child to encompass and contain his sensations by gathering him up and enfolding him in her arms, soothingly and comfortably. And then all the inner turmoil which bewildered him, threatened to engulf him, or to tear him to pieces, becomes, through mother, a manageable feeling, sometimes a good one, sometimes a not good one, but bearable all the same. As the parents accompany their empathy and support with words, they give their child names for their own and his feelings—happy, angry, sad, hurt. These names help the child to form a mental symbol, an idea, of the sensations he experiences. The word gives them shape within himself, holds them together, perhaps not unlike the way the parents' arms around him held them together, and in time, when he can say these words, they also serve him as mental channels of discharge which facilitate mastery (Katan, 1961; E. Furman, 1992, 1993). In this way feelings increasingly become a mental function. They remain in tune with the body and inform us about it, but provide a mental way of experiencing, mastering, and discharging. This protects our bodily processes from stress and enables us to control our actions.

A child's ability to feel, and to tolerate his feelings, depends for a long time on being felt with by mother, and also by father, and on their help in containing his feelings. When a toddler, and even a preschooler, has a strong feeling, he first looks to the parents, checking whether they mirror his feeling, whether they feel with him, how they contain it, and if need be, he gets their help with it: through a nod, facial expression, through their words, or a hug. Young children often cannot feel at all unless the parent feels with them and unless they can rely on him or her to help contain the feeling.

Twenty-two-month-old Pat, well developed and lively, attended a day care center. He had formed a trusting relationship with Ms. G., his caregiver, whom he shared with a few other youngsters. One day Ms. G. noticed that Pat was a little quiet and occasionally flapped one ear with his hand. She surmised that something was wrong but, although he had often come for help to her with minor complaints, he did not respond to her sympathetic questions and showed no affect. She phoned his mother to come and get him and was glad that Pat willingly curled up on her lap while they waited. As soon as Pat saw his mom in the door, he ran into her open arms and sobbed bitterly as she held and comforted him. It turned out that Pat was suffering from an ear infection and had obviously been in considerable pain. In spite of his close relationship with his caregiver, however, he could not fully feel his pain or communicate it until he was with his mother (E. Furman, 1984a).

Susan and Joel, both twenty-four-months-old, attended a different day care center, where a large group of children and staff working in irregular shifts made a close relationship between child and caregiver very difficult to establish. Although Susan had been in the center for many months, she was distant and aloof, though conforming. Joel was a quiet newcomer. One day, Joel and Susan were sitting near each other when, out of the blue, Joel bit Susan's arm several times before the alarmed caregiver could separate them. It was striking that neither the attacker nor the victim showed or expressed any feeling before, during, or after the incident. There were no signs of anger, pain, or fear. Both looked blank and did not respond to the adult's concern, comfort, or reprimand. When the respective parents were informed at pick-up time, they did not address their children's feelings and the children still showed none. Susan's mother, always harried, responded with "She'll get over it. Serves her right anyway because she used to bite," and Joel's father merely rebuked him. When the day care staff discussed the incident and their own upset with their consultant, they recalled that Susan had never shown feelings at the center or when observed with her mother, and that Joel had not expressed the expectable upset and anger during his recent separation–adjustment period. The children's inability to feel seemed not only related to their insufficiently close relationships with the staff but to their parents' inability to feel with them. Susan's mother could not feel with her daughter's pain or possible anger and could not comfort her. Joel's father could not feel that his son must have been angry to bite, much less inquire what he might have been angry about. Their experience with other youngsters led the staff to suspect that Joel was angry at the adults, at his parents and at them, for being left at the center. They embarked on an ultimately rather successful program of helping these children to feel and of helping their parents to feel with them. Susan learned to use her feelings to protect herself, and Joel, once able to feel his anger and express it in words, could better control his aggressive actions.

Even grown-ups need someone to share and contain their feelings when the stress is unusual. Mr. Z., a twenty-one-year-old student, recalled a recent car accident from which he barely escaped unhurt. He called the police, the tow truck, took care of everything, and then phoned his parents. As soon as he heard his father's concerned, "I am so sorry," he realized just how scared and upset he was, burst into tears and shared his feelings, relieved because he knew his father understood.

Often though, even with much less powerful feelings, we continue to need an empathic sharer and container: "This makes me so happy, I can't wait to get home and tell my family," or "This is just so maddening, I'll have to tell them all about it at home." To feel and be felt with is not only part of the parent–child relationship. Later on, it becomes a vital part of every friendship. A true friend is one who can feel with us, listen sympathetically, and not be "thrown" by our feelings but help us to bear, contain, and master them so that we gain a measure of relief.

As the child's capacity to feel increases, his feelings become less closely tied to the body. Now even intense pleasure can be felt and contained before it becomes overwhelming and unbearably "bad." This does not always hold, as parents of schoolchildren well know when they call out to them, "Stop all that excited laughing and running around! Now it's still fun, but soon you'll be crying and complaining." Unpleasurable feelings can also be endured better, though even schoolchildren may still need to be reminded, "Now come on, this is a little hurt. You don't need to carry on quite that much about it!" At the same time, both good and bad feelings become more varied and finely shaded, and acquire specific and different meanings. There is annoyed, angry, furious; there is disappointed, sad, lonely, helpless, envious, and jealous. There is a wide range of pleasant feelings—comfortable, happy, delighted, excited, pleased. All along, the parents help by feeling with their child and by giving him the words to name and express what is felt. When talking about feelings with each other is part of the parent–child relationship, young children often invent their own terms to describe their or the parent's feelings. One two-and-a-half-year-old accurately told his pleased-feeling mother, "You have a smile inside today"; another youngster watched her brother dashing about irritably to collect his things and she commented, "Tommy has the angry jumpies." When children are able to feel, they can also feel with others. Their observations of themselves and of others are often stunningly penetrating, disarmingly frank, thoughtful and wise. Some adults may be taken aback by such comments and laugh with embarrassment which humiliates children, but parents who respect their children's feelings take them seriously and respond to them in kind. They even find their children helpful and value them as friends, because they can share and understand so much so deeply—sometimes more so than other adults.

SOME WAYS IN WHICH PARENTS ARE NOT HELPFUL WITH FEELINGS

When parents really help their children with feelings, they help them to experience feelings, to contain and tolerate them, and to discharge them mainly through thought and speech. They do not ignore their children's feelings, nor do they confuse them or take them away. But parents themselves may not have been helped with feelings when they were little and their attitudes may get in the way of helping their children.

Sometimes parents are not in tune and cannot feel with their baby or young child. Then they cannot mirror correctly what he feels and, as a result, cannot help him to contain what he experiences and give it mental shape and content. The infant finds no echo in their faces, voices or movements, no pattern for structuring and mastering what goes on within him. He may then not learn to build a meaningful link between sensations and feelings. His feelings may remain primitively labile and overwhelming, or they may become blank, dull, and flat, or they may take the form of vague chronic moods, irritable, anxious, or excitable. In either case, they will fail truly to reflect and crystallize his inner experience, while his discharges continue to be channeled through bodily processes and behavioral manifestations.

Sometimes parents do feel with their child but are unable to contain the feelings and to give them controlled mental expression. Instead, they become as frantic or excited as the child and so overwhelmed by what they feel that they too may resort to mainly bodily discharges: shrieking and waving arms, or tensing up and turning rigid, or fussing and bustling aimlessly. Children may come to do likewise with their feelings, or they may shy away from having feelings altogether because their overwhelmed and overwhelming parents scare them.

Some parents are quite content to assist their children with good feelings, comfortable and happy ones, but find it hard to help them with "bad" feelings, pain, sadness, or anger. They may wish to spare their children discomfort, may wish to avoid feeling guilty at having caused it, contributed to it, or failed to prevent it, and they may also wish to avoid reciprocating their youngsters' feelings, such as getting angry at the child who is angry at them. They may also feel that, on moral grounds, nobody should entertain "bad" feelings. Whatever the reason, it affects their tolerance and support of the child's unpleasant feelings.

Parents may ignore the child's feeling and try to suppress its behavioral manifestations, like Susan's mother and Joel's father in our earlier illustration. As we later learned through working with these parents, they could not recognize or help their children recognize pain and anger because they could not bear their own discomfort at having left them, exposed them to unhappiness, and caused them to be sad and angry. As long as the children did not feel anything, the parents did not need to feel bad. These parents therefore did not connect the children's behavior with feelings and actually ordered the children not to express feelings through their behavior: no biting, no crying. As soon as the parents could be helped to feel their own uncomfortable feeling, guilt, they could also help their children feel theirs, loneliness and anger.

Some parents sense that the child would show his feelings if he were with them and they stay away from him in the hope that the feelings will disappear if there is no opportunity to show them. For example, mothers may leave without saying good-bye to their children ("sneaking away"), they may arrange for father or another adult to transport their child to and from nursery school or day care center. They may not accompany their child to the doctor, and they may not visit him in the hospital, all in order to avoid tears or anger. In these instances, the parents, and other adults, often mistake the cart for the horse. They assume that the parent's presence causes the child's feelings, rather than that the feelings are there but cannot be felt and contained except in the presence of the parent. It looks to them as if the child felt fine until the parent upset him: "He stopped crying the moment mother left and was okay from then on." "It's not good for him to get so upset, so it would be better if you didn't visit him." The child who does not show and verbalize unhappy feelings because there is no one there to feel with him is not okay. He is merely deprived of becoming aware of his feelings and of gradually mastering them through words with the help of the loved parent.

Some parents so much want their child to have only good feelings that they superimpose a happy feeling on his unhappy one. When the infant cries or looks distressed and angry, they laugh and bounce and tickle him to get him to laugh too; when their toddler or preschooler is angry and complains about his parents' going out, they persuade him how much fun he'll have with the baby-sitter or how exciting it will be to stay up late and watch more TV. When his pet fish dies they quickly buy a new and bigger one so that, instead of being sad, he will be thrilled with owning something better. When there is a scary story or program, they pretend it's really funny and merits hilarity. Such children's "happy" feelings are shrill, brittle, and false. False feelings cut us off from what goes on within us, instead of helping us to cope with it. False feelings may also cut us off from others because we cannot feel with others without being in good touch with our own feelings, and because others regard false feelings as inappropriate; for example, some children, and even adults, giggle when they see a handicapped person, smile when reprimanded, or tell funny jokes on sad occasions.

But even when parents feel with their child and comfort him, their comfort is not helpful if intended to smooth over and stop his feelings: "Hush, hush, it's all better now," "You're not sad anymore, are you?" Comfort works best when it alleviates distress enough to make it manageable and when it offers ways of appropriate expressions, mainly verbal expression, accompanied by the limited bodily discharge associated with feelings—frowning, smiling, laughing, crying, posture, movements. This constitutes mastery.

WHEN FEELINGS SEEM DANGEROUS TO CHILDREN

Children's difficulties with tolerating and mastering feelings are by no means simply due to parental handling. Considerable obstacles within the child work against his ability to live with feelings. *We* may know of the many ways in which feelings are useful and enriching to the personality, but to the child, and the young child especially, they are often a menace.

In infancy and during the toddler years, when tolerance is still limited, feelings easily become "too big." Then they overwhelm, or threaten to overwhelm, an experience most babies have endured at times. Older persons sometimes describe it: "It came rushing up like a tidal wave."; "It made me feel like I was about to explode." The very young child is always close to the danger that his feelings will have him instead of he having them. And so he, though notoriously oblivious to dangers from the outside (the ones grown-ups call the "real" dangers), keenly senses this inner danger which is so real to him The mothering person who is in tune with her child senses his vulnerability. This enables her to protect him, and to calm and contain his feelings for him. In doing so she helps the child to develop his own stamina for feelings, but, in the meantime and until he can really trust his own ability to keep his feelings within manageable limits (and that's a long time!), the child depends on her availability. This is a very important reason why very young children need their mothers always to be there and why it is so difficult for them to accept a substitute. They are not worried that their needs will not be met, or that they will fall ill, or that the house will burn down. They worry that they will be at the mercy of their sensations and feelings, stemming from whatever cause, which only mother can empathize with and "tame." The mere idea of being without mother makes the feelings seem potentially more dangerous. It is a bit like when we start to swim in deep water before we are really sure of our swimming skills. If someone we trust is nearby and watches out for us, it's not half as scary as when we are all on our own, or when we are not sure that whoever is there really knows that we may need help and could really rescue us in case of need. But even this is not a very good simile. It leaves out the very little child's limited ability to communicate and understand which makes him much more helpless, and it leaves out the fact that when mother is not available, the child's longing, sadness, and anger at missing her as a loved one already greatly tax his feeling capacity.

When mother is not there, or is there but does not help them with their feelings, some children indeed become overwhelmed with dread and distress, while others, toddlers especially, often "act up" or bother mother "to get attention," letting her know in this way that they feel the inner danger rising. From the second half of the first year on, however, youngsters also avoid the danger of too big feelings by not having feelings at all. This is not their deliberate decision. It is a protective device, perhaps like an anesthetic which frees us from experiencing what is happening to us. When a child copes in this manner, mother is not likely to notice that the child is bothered by her unavailability, and, if she was actually absent, she is apt to hear "He was fine. Didn't even notice you were gone." This may be helpful to the child for a while, may keep him going and enable him to postpone feeling until it is safe, until mother returns and is there to help. However, when feelings are banished from awareness most of the time because they seem too dangerous, the child cannot develop his ability to tolerate and master them and they cannot come to serve him.

Usually, parents try to protect their child from being left alone with "too big" feelings. That is why they try to adjust the time spans of their absences or unavailability to the child's tolerance for feelings and, all along, help him with them to increase his mastery; for example, mother may encourage the child to share his feelings before she leaves, and make this a part of preparing him for her absence. She may likewise encourage and accept his feelings on her return, "Well, how did it go? Was it hard?" She may let him know, as best as possible, just how long she will be gone, may leave "a bit of Mom" with him to keep (her old purse, scarf, key case), and if she thinks her absence may exceed his limit, she may periodically check in to talk with him by phone. Moreover, she tries to use sitters who have the kind of relationship with the child which will enable them to help him with his feelings, who will empathize with and support his feelings, including those related to the missing mother. But parents help a lot even just by understanding how scary big feelings can be, and by letting the child know they understand, as well as by assuring him that it will get easier to handle as he gets older.

Children are not only afraid that feelings may get too big. They also do not like the discomfort of unpleasant feelings, are not eager to feel them, and are apt to shy away from them even when the parents are there and would help: "It doesn't bother me."; "I am not scared."; "I don't miss my mom."; "I don't care, I'm not mad." Sometimes not feeling extends to not noticing the situation which may engender feelings; for example, a toddler may avoid noticing mother's preparations for leaving, may not seem to hear her goodbye, give no indication of thinking about her after she is gone, and pay no attention to her return, as if she had never left at all. It is always tempting for the caring adults to leave sleeping lions alone, and be glad there was no fuss, but many mothers are aware that the child will be better off in the long run if they remind him of the reality and of his feelings about it and they help him to make them, if not pleasant, at least bearable. Thus, when parents notice that the child avoids difficult feelings in situations which warrant them, they encourage him to let himself feel them, and to learn that they can be mastered. "You didn't like to hear that I'll be going out, did you? It's all right not to like it. It's even all right not to like mom." Or, "It's hard when I'm busy with the baby. I am sorry. You can tell me." Or "I know it feels bad when I scold you. It's okay to feel bad. Mom and dad also sometimes feel bad."

In time feelings threaten in yet another way when the wishes and fantasies that accompany them seem to endanger the loved ones who are the child's protector, or seem to threaten the relationships with them, or are thought to provoke possible retaliation from them. When older toddlers or preschoolers get very angry at Mom and, in their anger, want to hurt her, send her away, no longer love her or have anything to do with her because she is "so mean," they worry that this may really happen, or that she will get so angry back that she will no longer care for them, or that she might even do to them the very things they want to do to her. When Mom then gets angry at them for some reason, or happens to fall ill, or has to leave, they easily see it as the consequence of their own anger. Similarly, when their loving feelings for Dad, Grandma, or sitter get very strong, they often fear that their disloyalty will leave too little love for Mom, that they may wish to have the other person for their new mom and reject the old mom altogether, and that Mom may do likewise unto them. She may love her job or her new baby better than them and abandon them. Some children cling to mother and dare not like nursery school lest they get to like it too much. Some, for the same reason, test their mother's response by letting her know that they like someone else better and want to stay with him or her. Envy can be felt as threatening when the child wants to take away the parents' desirable attributes and possessions and fears their anger and retaliation; and so can jealousy, when the child cannot bear to be left out of the parents' partnership and when his intense love for one parent makes him want to take the place of the other one. (Supposing that other parent, who is so much bigger and stronger, gets wind of it and pays him back?)

Again, parents help. They reassure the child that the wishes and thoughts that go with feelings don't come true and that they would not let the child act on them: "You can feel angry and wish mean things but they won't really happen." (Children don't always like that reassurance; some say, "But *my* wishes do come true because I can wish so hard!") Parents explain that coincidental events are related to causes other than the child's feelings. "I am not going to work because you were mad at me or because I am mad at you, but because I need to earn money to buy food and clothes and toys." And they also reassure that they do not harbor similar feelings and/or that they will not retaliate: "It's okay to like nursery school. You'll still like me and I'll still like you and you'll always be my little girl. And when I'm at work—or with the baby—I still think of you and I don't like work—or the baby—better than you." Or "I know you'd like to have my things, but I won't really let you take them and when I get angry at you I won't hurt you or take away your things."

WHAT HAPPENS TO UNRECOGNIZED FEELINGS?

How do children themselves deal with feelings which seem dangerous? After all, they do not always become overwhelmed, they do not always want mother right there so she can help in case their feelings get out of hand, nor do they always tell us, "I'm afraid I'm going to be too angry," or "I'll get to love Grandmother too much when she takes care of me," or "I'll get too envious and want to steal your things." We know already that very young children who cannot experience feelings consciously tend to continue to discharge sensations through bodily processes, or revert to that. Indeed, young children's frequent troubles with eating, sleeping, toileting, and other interferences with their bodily needs and well-being are often a sign that they cannot cope with their feelings. We also know already that children often bypass being aware of their feelings and, instead, discharge them through actions. They may bite, hit, or destroy things without feeling angry; they may take others' possessions without being aware of feeling envious, or insist on sleeping in the parents' bed without recognizing that they feel jealous and left out.

But these are not their only ways of coping. Often children do become very scared but of something outside of themselves. Instead of an inside danger which is so hard to pinpoint, to contain, and to get away from, their fears focus on an outside danger which is relatively safer—you can locate and control it better and you can hide from it more effectively. Dangerous feelings thus turn into irrational fears.

Toddlers, who often struggle with big angry feelings, tend to be afraid of things that sound very loud and hence angry: thunder, big machines, garbage trucks, vacuum cleaners. Some parents try to reassure their youngsters that these things are safe; some try to explain intellectually how they work. The most helpful approach is to tell the child what they are not, that these things are not angry and don't act out of anger. Two-year-old Marilyn was terrified of the siren noise made by ambulance and police cars. Her parents' patient explanations about them hurrying to help people proved of no avail. One day Marilyn's mother disappointed her and the little girl responded by imitating a siren noise herself, right near her mother's face. "I think you are very angry," said her mother, "I wish you'd tell me instead of making this terrible noise." After a moment's thought though, she added "Now I understand why you are so scared of sirens! I guess you think they are as angry as you are! But they are not angry at all, they just make a big noise so all the cars can hear them and will stop to let them go ahead." Marilyn looked a bit sheepish and buried her head in Mom's lap. It was the end of her fear of sirens. Of course, some of the things the children fear, such as a thunderstorm, may be dangerous and the children may have heard that, but this reality accounts only for part of their fear. The anger they attribute to it makes it seem much more dangerous. As the young child is helped to tolerate, master, and express his feelings more appropriately, these early fears usually subside (E. Furman, 1992, 1993).

The preschoolers' irrational fears are more elaborate and sophisticated and may include several worrisome ideas, but basically they too represent the child's unconscious mental attempt to substitute a "safer" fear for one less safe, an outside danger for one which stems from his feelings and wishes. Ronny, aged four, was quite scared of robbers and insisted on closing his windows and locking all doors at night: "A robber might come and take all our things." His mother noticed that Ronny often greeted Dad lately in a disgruntled mood and borrowed Dad's hat and briefcase to impersonate him after dinner. This gave her the idea that perhaps Ronny himself had some "take away" envious feelings. She shared her idea with her son and asked him just exactly what the robber would take if he came into their home. "All of daddy's money," replied Ronny, adding, "Don't you know he puts all his silver coins on the dresser at night?" Dad did indeed put his change on the dresser. When mother wondered whether perhaps Ronny had "robber wishes" for Dad's money, the boy blurted out, "And I did, I took two of his silver." It turned out that Ronny had hidden away two of Dad's dimes, and was plagued by guilt and fear of what Dad would do to him in retaliation. The dimes were returned to Dad. Dad told Ronny that he could well understand his wanting to take Dad's things to be big because he used to feel that way about his dad when he was still little. But whereas wanting to take away was all right, really doing it was not, and Ronny would need to do his own growing to get big and that would take time. Ronny felt relieved and was no longer afraid of robbers. When Ronny, like many other youngsters, could not acknowledge and cope with his infantile envy, his feelings were in part expressed in actions and in part "given" to an imaginary robber who at least could be controlled with the help of locks.

Real events, experienced or heard of, play their part. They may trigger the child's fear, they may confirm his imagined dangers, they may provide a plausible content, or they may contribute elements of "outside" fear to "inside" fear. Real events also arouse feelings on their own account and inevitably add to the amount of feelings a child has to cope with. Parents help by limiting their children's exposure to experiences which are likely to intensify their feelings beyond bearable limits. But when their child develops an exaggerated or irrational fear they usually sense that something is troubling him and that their best chance of helping is to figure out with him what causes it, perhaps by asking the child to tell them more about it: What will the monster do? Why would it do just that? How does it look? Sometimes parents hear surprising but ultimately enlightening answers.

Three-and-a-half-year-old Sheila had become very scared of the weekly garbage collection. She was already anxious when mother prepared the bags of rubbish the night before; she often could not sleep lest the truck come early; when she heard it she quickly hid away and then peeked furtively through the window to make sure it had left. In response to mother's inquiries, Sheila voiced her awe at how big it was and how much could be put into it. "It really takes away everything," she marveled, "and it never brings anything back, does it?" "Well, it only takes what people put out. That's its job." "But sometimes people make mistakes. Remember when you threw away dad's letter and he never found it and he was mad." Yes, mother remembered that, and she suddenly also remembered that, many months ago, when Sheila's little brother was born, Sheila had offered to bring him downstairs to be put out with the garbage "because it was time to send him away again." Mother had assured her that he would stay with them and that there was enough love for both of them. In time, Sheila had seemed to have gotten to like him and played with him. As if guessing mother's thought, Sheila said "Mommy, they don't take children by mistake, do they?" This clarified matters and mother could now assure Sheila that parents don't get rid of children, even when they are very angry and want to be mean, like sending away their little brothers or anyone else. Sheila gave Mommy a hug. Mother realized that Sheila had not coped with her anger as well as it had looked. She helped Sheila recognize and master it better, piecemeal, as suitable situations turned up. Sheila responded and that made her harder to live with for quite some time, but her fear subsided, and eventually she was master in her own house of many feelings.

Sheila's, like all children's, irrational or exaggerated fear did make sense once it could be understood. Oftentimes parents can and do enlist their child's help in the process.

Although fears can protect children to some extent from the danger of their feelings, their minds use also other protective devices which enable them to feel even more comfortable. Again, they are not measures they choose to employ, but measures that operate unconsciously when an inner danger becomes too threatening. There are as many such mechanisms as there are individuals, but some are widely used and we have already come across a few of them. One we illustrated in connection with the child not noticing when mother prepared to leave. Like the proverbial ostrich, these children may be "blind" to situations that are likely to cause them dangerous feelings. We have also talked about children who substitute a happy feeling for an unhappy one, such as smiling when reprimanded or cracking jokes when there is reason to be sad. They may also "love" injections and scary movies. Similarly, instead of feeling painfully helpless, toddlers may turn into powerful little dictators, and little boys who feel inferior may, perhaps with the help of cowboy boots and toy guns, impress themselves and others with their "machismo." We have also mentioned children who, with or without parental encouragement, misdirect their feelings and vent them on "safer" targets, such as being angry at the baby, or at other little children, instead of at their parents. Children may also exchange one cause for another; for example, it may feel safer to be unhappy because "they canceled my favorite TV program" than to be unhappy because Grandma is ill or because Dad is out of town.

Often children attribute their unwanted feelings to others, as happened with Ronny; we also talked about such children seeing their own anger in the parents and experiencing the parents as much "meaner" and more punitive than they really are. Sadness, and other feelings too, may be seen only in others but go unrecognized in the child himself. "My sister cries and cries because we had to give away our dog, but I don't mind."

These and other inner protections against feelings may be helpful to an extent, but if they are used persistently and widely, even in situations that could be mastered, and if they interfere considerably with recognizing and tolerating feelings, then they become a real danger. They cause troubles of their own. They cut the child off from his feelings and make it impossible for him to master and use them. They may get him into difficulties. (Supposing he doesn't notice an oncoming car because he would get too scared if he saw it!) Worst of all, perhaps, they may interfere with his development: Every phase in personality development requires that we come to terms with its special emotional tasks. We can only accomplish that by experiencing and mastering the feelings connected with them: be it accepting himself as a boy or herself as a girl, or having to come to terms with having to grow up slowly and bearing frustrations in the meantime, or coming to terms with being grown-up and having to renounce some of our attachments to our parents. In addition, life may bring unexpected trials and hardships whose attendant feelings also have to be endured and mastered. When children do not have their feelings available, they cannot master these tasks and are in danger of "getting stuck." Their personality development may be interfered with because their energies may continue to be tied up in battling old conflicts instead of being free to deal with the problems of the present.

Parents are usually not aware of these dangers but they sense when their child is not in touch with his feelings and cannot share them. They often have a feel for when, defensively, he is "putting it on too thick." They may well recognize the underlying unwanted feelings and try to make them more acceptable for him; for example, when "only sister" cries for the family dog, Dad may say, "Well, I am sad for him too. We all loved him and it would be strange if we did not miss him." Many parents interfere when the child's way of warding off feelings gets in the way of daily behavior; for example, when their little boy insists on wearing his cowboy boots and toy gun to nursery school all the time, the parents may ask him to dispense with them sometimes and say something like: "Most boys want to look big and strong, especially when they are still new at nursery school and aren't so sure what the other kids will think of them. It's always hard at first to be in a new place but the boots and gun won't really make it all right. In time you'll feel better when you learn to do well all the things they do at school, and then the others will also think well of you."

WHAT HAPPENS WHEN CHILDREN KEEP THEIR FEARS? DO THEY EVENTUALLY OUTGROW THEM?

Some fears do subside as the child learns to tolerate his feelings better, resolves developmental conflicts of one phase, and progresses to the next. Sometimes, however, the outcome is not so constructive. One fear may pass, only to be replaced by another one, or the fear may pass but another, apparently unrelated, difficulty may arise instead. For example, a child may then need to ward off all feelings; or his bodily needs may suffer interference with sleep, eating, or toileting problems; or a restriction in functioning, such as a learning trouble, may replace the fear; or a difficulty in relationships may intensify, such as getting into squabbles and arguments or feeling disliked; or the child may remain emotionally "immature," may fail to face and cope with the developmental tasks of growing up. These maladaptive solutions indicate that the child could not come to terms with the "dangerous" feelings that caused his earlier fear and that they continue to burden him unduly.

It is sometimes difficult to know at the time whether the child will or will not be able to master the "dangerous" feelings that his fear signals. When the fear is intense, goes on for some time, and interferes with the child's daily life, chances are he has trouble coping. Parents help best by seeking professional advice. A stitch in time saves nine—understanding and resolving children's fears during their preschool years is much easier and more effective, and prevents further interferences in personality growth. Symptoms related to these emotional difficulties can also be treated later, but it is inevitably harder and takes longer.

WHEN PEOPLE DISCHARGE THEIR FEELINGS THROUGH BODILY PROCESSES, DO THEY HAVE PSYCHOSOMATIC ILLNESSES?

The early closeness between body and feelings is normal and even if it persists it causes various forms of bodily distress but not *psychosomatic illness*. The latter term is usually reserved for cases where a bodily anomaly or weakness exists that either causes bodily symptoms or is so vulnerable that it starts to give rise to symptoms when subjected to additional stress from any source. The psychological factor in true psychosomatic illness is always secondary and may operate in two ways: (1) The affected bodily organ may provide a readily available channel for bodily discharge of sensations and feelings. This may make it harder for feelings to become a mainly mental function, just as it would be harder to divert a stream of water along a new pathway when there is a leak en route which drains it off. At the same time, as the sensations and feelings continue to be "sidetracked" and discharged through the affected organ (skin, breathing apparatus, intestines, etc.), they aggravate its condition and worsen the symptoms. (2) Feelings, especially "dangerous" feelings, may constitute one of the stresses which overtax the vulnerable affected organ so that its malfunction causes manifest symptoms (R. A. Furman, 1969).

Psychological treatment of psychosomatic illnesses does not cure the somatic anomaly or weakness. It can help to reduce the stress, if the stress is of a psychological nature, and/or to divert feelings from the area of bodily discharge into a mental pathway, where the person can then be aware of them and discharge them primarily through thought and speech.

WHY IS IT SO BAD NOT TO HAVE "BAD" FEELINGS?

We need all our feelings to serve us. Even the "bad" ones are of help; for example, sadness helps us to keep in mind our loved ones when they are absent, anger helps us to stand up for ourselves, helplessness may help us to resign ourselves, if need be. Recognizing our own "bad" feelings also helps us to feel with others when they have them, and enables us to deepen our relationships with them—a good-times-only friend is not a real friend.

Last, but not least, unpleasant feelings also help us by contrast to enjoy and appreciate the pleasant ones. It happens not infrequently that when people "do away" with their "bad" feelings, their "good" ones become blunted or lost as well.

NEEDS, URGES, AND FEELINGS

Basic Concepts

• The innate vital energy of every personality manifests itself in needs, urges, and feelings.

• When appropriately mastered, they contribute to health, growth, and richness in all areas of functioning.

• Needs, urges, and feelings undergo many changes in the course of development, as do the child's means of controlling and gratifying them.

• Parents and other adults facilitate this development.

An Afterthought

Have you asked yourself, as so many have, this question: Why have we talked so much about children's early life and so little about when they are older? Don't many people other than their parents influence their development in those later years, and isn't that part of their development just as important?

When we look at a building we see all its parts above the ground, but not its foundation. We rarely even think about its foundation, and when we do occasionally see it during construction, it appears dull, uninteresting, and unimportant. We can't wait for the "real" building, the upper visible structure, to take shape, so that we will know what it is all about. We forget that the foundation is the most crucial part, that it determines what can be built up and whether what is built on it will hold up.

The child's early years are his foundation, buried and out of view, forgotten by himself and often disregarded by others, along with the raw materials he contributed and the parents' work which helped to mold them together into a coherent whole. The later years, the years of building the visible structure of the personality, are more readily open to view, as are those who participate in giving it its final shape.

We have been looking at what goes on when the foundation is laid.

References

Freud, A. (1949a), Aggression in relation to emotional development. *The Psychoanalytic Study of the Child*, 3/4:37–42. New York: International Universities Press.

—— (1949b), Notes on aggression. In: *The Writings of Anna Freud*, 4:60–74. New York: International Universities Press, 1968.

Freud, S. (1916), Criminals from a sense of guilt. *Standard Edition*, 14:332–333. London: Hogarth Press, 1957.

Furman, E. (1980), Early latency—Normal and pathological aspects. In: *The Course of Life. Psychoanalytic Contributions Toward Understanding Personality Development*, Vol. 2, ed. S. I. Greenspan & G. H. Pollock. Washington, DC: NIMH, pp. 1–32.

—— (1981), Children with toddler-like behavior in the nursery school. In: *What Nursery School Teachers Ask Us About: Psychoanalytic Consultations in Preschools*, ed. E. Furman. Madison, CT: International Universities Press, 1986, pp. 149–164. Also Pamphlet Series of the Cleveland Center for Research in Child Development, 2084 Cornell Road, Cleveland, Ohio 44106.

—— (1982a), Mothers have to be there to be left. *The Psychoanalytic Study of the Child*, 37:15–28. New Haven, CT: Yale University Press.

—— (1982b), On discipline in the Nursery School. In: *What Nursery School Teachers Ask Us About: Psychoanalytic Consultations in Preschools*, ed. E. Furman. Madison, CT: International Universities Press, 1986, pp. 69–87. Also Pamphlet Series of the Cleveland Center for Research in Child Development, 2084 Cornell Road, Cleveland, Ohio 44106.

—— (1984a), Mothers, toddlers and care. In: *ERIC, ED 256 479*. Urbana, IL: University of Illinois at Urbana-Champaign, 1985.

Also Pamphlet Series of the Cleveland Center for Research in Child Development, 2084 Cornell Road, Cleveland, Ohio 44106.

———— (1984b), Some difficulties in assessing depression and suicide in childhood and adolescence. In: *Suicide in the Young*, ed. H. S. Sudak, A. B. Ford, & N. B. Rushforth. Littleton, MA: Wright P.S.G., pp. 245–258.

———— (1985), Learning to feel good about sexual differences. In: *What Nursery School Teachers Ask Us About: Psychoanalytic Consultations in Preschoolers*. Madison, CT: International Universities Press, 1986, pp. 101–122. Also Pamphlet Series of the Cleveland Center for Research in Child Development, 2084 Cornell Road, Cleveland, Ohio 44106.

———— (1987a), *Helping Young Children Grow*. Madison, CT: International Universities Press.

———— (1987b), *The Teacher's Guide to Helping Young Children Grow*. Madison, CT: International Universities Press.

———— (1992), *Toddlers and Their Mothers*. Madison, CT: International Universities Press.

———— (1993), *Toddlers and Their Mothers: Abridged Version for Parents and Educators*. Madison, CT: International Universities Press.

———— (1994a), Early aspects of mothering: What makes it so hard to be there to be left. *J. Child Psychother.*, 20(2):149–164.

———— (1994b), *On Liking Oneself: Development of Self Esteem*. Pamphlet Series of the Cleveland Center for Research in Child Development, 2084 Cornell Road, Cleveland, Ohio 44106. Also in *Preschoolers: Questions and Answers—Psychoanalytic Consultations with Parents, Teachers and Caregivers*, ed. E. Furman. Madison, CT: International Universities Press, 1995, pp. 19–36.

———— (1998a), *Relationships in Early Childhood: Helping Young Children Grow*. Madison, CT: International Universities Press.

———— (1998b), *Self-Control and Mastery in Early Childhood: Helping Young Children Grow*. Madison, CT: International Universities Press.

Furman, R. A. (1969), Psychosomatic disorders. In: *The Therapeutic Nursery School*, ed. R. A. Furman & A. Katan. New York: International Universities Press, pp. 231–273.

———— (1983), The father-child relationship. In: *What Nursery School Teachers Ask Us About: Psychoanalytic Consultations in Preschools*, ed. E. Furman. Madison, CT: International Universities Press, 1986, pp. 21–34. Also Pamphlet Series of the Cleveland Center for Research in Child Development, 2084 Cornell Road, Cleveland, Ohio 44106.

—— (1991), *On Toilet Mastery*. Pamphlet Series of the Cleveland Center for Research in Child Development, 2084 Cornell Road, Cleveland, Ohio 44106. Also *Child Analysis*, 1993, 4:62–74. Also in *Preschoolers: Questions and Answers—Psychoanalytic Consultations with Parents, Teachers and Caregivers*, ed. E. Furman. Madison, CT: International Universities Press, 1995, pp. 109–121.

—— (1994), Helping children cope with stress. Pamphlet Series of the Cleveland Center for Research in Child Development, 2084 Cornell Road, Cleveland, Ohio 44106. Also in *Preschoolers: Questions and Answers—Psychoanalytic Consultations with Parents, Teachers and Caregivers*, ed. E. Furman. Madison, CT: International Universities Press, pp. 51–64.

—— Furman, E. (1984), Intermittent decathexis—A type of parental dysfunction. *Internat. J. Psycho-Anal.*, 65:423–433.

Hall, R. (1982a), Living with Spiderman et al.—Mastering aggression and excitement. In: *What Nursery School Teachers Ask Us About: Psychoanalytic Consultations in Preschools*, ed. E. Furman. Madison, CT: International Universities Press, 1986, pp. 89–99.

—— (1982b), Helping children with speech. In: *What Nursery School Teachers Ask Us About: Psychoanalytic Consultations in Preschools*, ed. E. Furman. Madison, CT: International Universities Press, 1986, pp. 125–126. Also Pamphlet Series of the Cleveland Center for Research in Child Development, 2084 Cornell Road, Cleveland, Ohio 44106.

Katan, A. (1961), Some thoughts about the role of verbalization in early childhood. *The Psychoanalytic Study of the Child*, 16:184–188. New York: International Universities Press.

Related Reading

A number of publications were referred to in the text and listed in the Reference Section, and a few more are offered for further reading, to amplify or illustrate some of the topics. Some may strike a familiar chord and fit in with your thinking and feeling; others may seem cumbersome or go against the grain. As with all that has been written in this book, you, the reader, will know best which items seem helpful and which to set aside.

Freud, A. (1946), Freedom from want in early education. In: *The Writings of Anna Freud*, 4:425–441. New York: International Universities Press, 1968.

——— (1947), The establishment of feeding habits. In: *The Writings of Anna Freud*, 4:442–457. New York: International Universities Press, 1968.

——— (1956), Psychoanalytic knowledge applied to the rearing of children. In: *The Writings of Anna Freud*, 5:265–280. New York: International Universities Press, 1969.

Furman, E., ed. (1986), *What Nursery School Teachers Ask Us About: Psychoanalytic Consultations in Preschools*. Madison, CT: International Universities Press.

——— (1992), *Toddlers and Their Mothers*: Madison, CT: International Universities Press.

——— (1993), *Toddlers and Their Mothers: Abridged Version for Parents and Educators*. Madison, CT: International Universities Press.

——— ed. (1995), *Preschoolers: Questions and Answers—Psychoanalytic Consultations with Parents, Teachers and Caregivers*. Madison, CT: International Universities Press.

O'Connor, F. (1935), My Oedipus complex. In: *Collected Stories*. New York: Vintage Books, 1982, pp. 282–292.

Payne, E. (1944), *Katy No-Pocket*. Boston: Houghton Mifflin Co. (a children's book).

Index